Passages Toward the Dark

Port Townsend

Passages Toward the Dark

Thomas McGrath

Copper Canyon Press   1982

Some of these poems have appeared in the following magazines: *Aegis, American Dialog, American Poetry Review, Another Chicago Magazine, Beloit Poetry Journal, Cafe Solo, The Cat and the Moon, Chicago Review, Choice, Crazy Horse, Dacotah Territory, Dakota Arts Quarterly, Far Point, Fervent Valley, Grove, Kayak, The Lamp in the Spine, Mainstream, Measure, Minnesota Review, Moons and Lion Tales, The Nation, New Letters, New Poets of the Red River, North Country, North Country Anvil, North Dakota Review, The Only Journal of the Tibetan Kite Society, Outcry, Panama Gold, Poetry, Poetry Now, Praxis, Preview, Puerto del Sol, Quetzal, Refugee Journal, road/house, San Marcos Review, Sez, Thunderbird, Uzzano, Voyages to the Inland Sea, Willow Springs.*

In addition to the editors of magazines where many of these poems were printed, I want to thank Robert Schuler of Uzzano Press for the right to republish *Waiting for the Angel* and *Open Songs* (both of them out of print) which appear in this book slightly rearranged and considerably amplified; and Jim Perlman of Holy Cow! Press for permission to include *Letters to Tomasito* which is printed here with added poems and in a form somewhat different from the original edition.

Some of the work on this book was made possible by grants from the Bush Foundation and the Minnesota State Arts Board.

Copper Canyon Press acknowledges the assistance of a grant from the National Endowment for the Arts. Special thanks to Centrum, where Copper Canyon is Press-in-Residence.

Thanks also to the poet Dale Jacobson for suggestions that led to the title of this book.

Copper Canyon Press
P.O Box 271
Port Townsend, WA 98368

ISBN 0-914742-63-9 (paper)
ISBN 0-914742-64-7 (cloth)

CONTENTS

I. Interfaces

II. Letters to Tomasito

III. Notes Taken During a Gunfight

IV. Open Songs

V. Half-time at the Funeral

VI. In Transit: Niño Perdido Toward Pah-Gatzin-Kay

for Tomasito

&

the Commune

I.

Interfaces

for Jack Beeching

DAWN SONG

The city lifts toward heaven from the continent of sleep
This skin of bricks,
                    these wounds,
                                   this soul of smoke and anguish,
These walls held up by hope and want, these right angles
Stony, where the familiar and the strange are joined:
                                                       tangential
Marriages.
            Imprisoned in the tall towers time kindles a ringing
Of iron bells.
                Iron round
                        bronze round
Resounding gongs clang in the nineteen tongues of the town
And the burnished sounds of the hours of dawn downsail and sing
Into the shadowy streets . . .
                              nightwater
                                          timesbourne . . .
                                                        Where we
Daily are borne, and dally our days along and sadly and gayly
Light up our candles in search of our hourly bread.

And now, putting off its suit of lights, its electric mythologies,
The platonic city floats up out of the dark:
                                              insubstantial
Structures, framework of dream and nightmare, a honeyed static
Incorporeal which the light condenses. A thin dust,
The fictions of time and custom, is clothing its mineral bones;

Out of the vapors of rent and habit the walls regain
Their untransparent strength; an ectoplasm of sweat and money
Crystallizes into roofs and docks; the bells collect
Around their bronze and song the cages of shimmering towers
And the footsteps of early workers are building the streets to the river.

THE LEGENDS

1.

Arrived there
They gathered flint for arrowheads
Before they knew if there were men
On the strange planet.

2.

When they came to the new world,
Some spent their whole lives
Looking for their own footprints.

3.

And so we are launched at last on the unknown river inland!
A book of salt for our guide,
Wampum of hardened tears for trade goods . . .
A lattice of dark crystals grows in the palm of my hand.

IN EARLY AUTUMN

On a day when the trees are exchanging the cured gold of the sun,
And the heavy oils of darkness in the rivers of their circular hearts
thicken;
       when desperation has entered the song of the locust;
When, in abandoned farmsites, the dark stays longer
In the closed parlor;
           a day when exhausted back-country roads,
Those barges loaded with sunlight and the bodies of dead animals,
Disappear into the Sand Hills under a swollen sun;
A day, too, when the sizzling flies are fingering their rosaries of blood
In the furry cathedrals of spent flesh, the left-over
Gone-green goners from the golden summer—

THEN I know a place with three dead dogs and two dead deer in one ditch.
I feel the displacement of minerals,
The stone grown fossils,
Under this hill of bones that calls my flesh its home.

IN SILENCE AND SOLITUDE

Night is entering the wood-lot
Like a secret clotting of blood:
The trees are coming to life
Out of darkness, solitude, hunger.
From his tunnel of sleep and snow
The field mouse is slowly pulled
By the deep tide of the trees,
By a polar silence, by terror . . .

Owl falls from air—
Not an owl: a command—
Down a long chute of feathers
(And under a spell of snow
The black book of a pinetree
Has closed a page on sleep,
On the lazy leather of birdsong)
—and the mouse has come to meet him!

Now the woods are dark—
For eyes as weak as a man's—
And the tale told in the snow
Is cold for the fault of sight.
But something sees and hears
Where mouse-print ended in screaming:
Aglow in the vault of night
The owl is dreaming.

THE SKULL OF THE HORSE

On the salt plaza
The ants hold court.
Beyond them,
Like a country of purest marble,
Stretch the lunar provinces.

In the empty eye holes,
The villages of the smallest tribesmen . . .
Their tents made of portable darkness
Their prince the prince of the dead.

THE RESTLESS NIGHT

Oh God help me now to cry out and bear witness;
Help me to send forth a great cry at the darkness;
Help me to waken my brother from his dream of rage and fire;
Help me to cry out in defence of my brother.
    Hush; do not let a moment's delirium
    Negate the decorum of a lifetime of indifference.
    If you should cry out there would be nothing to say.
    Hush; you would only waken the others.

Oh who among the bright hosts of the heavenly angels
Will call forward my name on a dark day?
Unless I cry forth to point my dark to the light,
To speak for my brother, that day who will call my name?
    Hush; do not let the temporary fever
    Astound the moment with its population of phantoms.
    You do not wish to appear ridiculous.
    Hush; there is really nothing you could say.

Oh if I do not rouse him who will awaken my brother
Dozing in this enduring instant of eternal damnation?
Sleepwalking in his immortality which is only lifelong—
Oh Watcher, help me to cry forth to my brother.
    Hush; do not let the guilt of a dark hour
    Breed the excess of revolutionary sympathy.
    Do not trust anguish; it is without function.
    Hush; the day comes: wherein no man speaks.

EASTER SONG

Why is it now I have to be born again
Mother? Isn't it—and if it isn't why isn't it—enough
That I ran round the world with my shoes full of holes?
Haven't I always drowned, punctual as a sack full of cats?

Nevertheless, here we are riding through Ransom County
With death in the back seat, just as if Dad were alive.
Ancient frightening machines resurrect through the Easter snow.
The bankers are flapping north in a cloud full of geese.

You won't talk, eh?—okay—so it's Good Friday
And we'll put in a crop as soon as they fix up the mortgage.
Old honey, give me your hand; I want to read the future
In that flesh map where every road leads West.

I know why you are dying and no doctor will tell you.
You have a little disease called America it has a southern accent
Irish ancestry German efficiency the know-how of a KC cathouse
It has loosed the fitful lightning of napalm on the dark girls of Selma

And Vietnam; and on you. And that's the reason our Old Man
Will never come home again, no matter how drunk he gets.
But the little super-nova the class struggle put in his belly will burn
As long as I live—longer, that is, than you'll see him in heaven.

—Only 6 o'clock in the morning and almost full light!
For whatever use they have for it. A killing light. Good Friday
Of our Lords of Phosphor-and-Cancer. Riding through Ransom County
We rise on revolutions of prayer wheels counting down death in your head

AFTERNOON OF A McGRATH
For my son Tomasito McGrath
after a visit to McGrath, Minnesota
(Aitken County)
early winter '74-'75

This morning there was one McGrath in Aitken County.
                                                    Now
There are three: the town, Tomasito, and myself.
                                    And at this rate of growth
The County will remain alive at least ten minutes longer,
Though the town is disappearing: fast: in a thickening snow:
Which is also the snow of time, the secret invisible snow
That falls in summer and falls in the fall and in spring: the snow
We are all disappearing into—all but Tomasito
Who has found a god-dog to mush home with if he knew where that was.

This town, which carries our name into the rising night,
Is one of those lost places in which I have found myself
Often . . . though they always had other names—and sometimes I did.
What could I expect to find in a place where the lakes hold only
Private water? A walk or a wake away from the Dead
Sea of Mille Lacs where all class-struggle is ethnic?
                                                    Place
Where each grave plot is bespoke and the loudest talk is on tombstones?
Did I think to push open a gate and enter a century of sleep
Where only myself is awake? But that's just the world I live in
Outside the township limits . . .
                            Perhaps I expected to find
Death McGrath, that stranger I meet so often in dreams,
The one I thought was myself disguised in the drag of death?
Perhaps he is one of these Indians, now in full retreat
(With their white comrades) from the shots and the double shots of General
Alcohol?
            But it's not the bargirl, inside whose head
It is snowing, as it snows in mine, and behind whose eyes I see
The slow turn to the left of those permanent low-pressure systems . . .

And that's McGrath. I will never forget it, now, Tomasito—
Our ghosts are here forever now because you were here
With this snow and this bar and that dog—see: what you have invented!
And so I will put this poem under a stone somewhere
On a road I will never walk on again, as I have done
Another time.
                    Or put it with our hidden wishing stone
To remember us by "forever": now: as the town disappears
Into the blizzard . . .
                    and all the McGraths drift into
That snow, that permanent white where all our colors fade.

The night is closing down. But I'd like McGrath to continue
Beyond this winter and those to come—though THAT beyond
Is beyond all hope.
                    So let me stop: here: then . . .
                                        —drifting
Into the universe and past all stars: toward those
Dark holes in space I must recognize as home.

THE DREAM RANGE

1.

When, young, I slept in a cold bed
My sleep was classical and calm.
The fallow field, the prunéd vine
The call of curlew and of kine—
These claimed and tuned my pastoral head:
I had no need for the dream range.

2.

My wife was softig and baroque,
But kept a hard board in the bed.
The burning colors of her day,
Eclipsing darkness cooled away.
Still, all that dark till I awoke,
I had the run of the dream range.

3.

From a dream of existential honey
I woke to voices crying *"more!"*—
Downpayments to save the nuptial manse
(From the fell clutch of low finance)
And gadgets might shame a metal whore—
And *that* was life on the dream range.

4.

Then Law came, like a walking turd,
Faith, Hope and Charity to divorce.
She kept the board, she kept the bed,
She kept the coldness in her head.
I paid for every loving word—O,
To hell! with life on the dream range!

LOVE SONG

1.

A time there was my true love changed,
Threw all my best books down the well,
Poisoned my son with a telling tale,
Set traps wherever my interest ranged.
Christ! (did I moan) Christ (did I sigh)
While the seely wench hoped I might die.
—Now that time's gone, and happily
I shout: Thank God I'm shed of thee!

2.

It seemed the moon fell from the sky;
And every bird froze on its bough.
By stormy cross ways must I go,
While her image, nailed to my inner eye,
Raged. O! lovers! have a care!
And bed not with the cold night mare!
Her glance will turn thy heart to stone
And freeze thy resurrection bone.

3.

But thankéd be this shinnying world!
For though one's haunted by a witch,
There's ways to shake the looney bitch
And many's the snug in the hoary cold!
Now thank thee, ladies, all and some,
Who laid me down and kept me warm—
Thy sweet devices, all, I praise.
And praise. And praise. And praise. And praise.

JOHN CAREY'S SECOND SONG

1.

The Hotel Peine Forte et Dure in Santa Monica
————and go in there:
Being too tired to drive home,
Or no home to drive to anyway.

2.

And go in there to the echoing fatigue in the thin sheets;
To wall paper held up by a kind of intramural
Desperation . . . out of the dark
Streets with their little flares of sex and drugs,
With the panhandlers and the drunks in the doorways,
At the end of the line, one jump away from salt water,
Beyond the riches of neon and the country of houses.

3.

And go in there.
This would be the end of the night except
This night has no end love has
No name this coffin has no handles
This room is, in its rationality,
A sort of end.

4.

But the end of the night? Now four hours
Until morning, the high workaday sun
Of unending midnight.
And go in there. And sleep.

ARCHETYPAL CATECHISM

Where are you running? the Old Man asks.
I am running toward hunger, the Child says.

Where are you running? the Child asks.
I am running toward thunder, the Young Man says.

Where are you running? the Young Man asks.
I am running toward lust, the Old Man says.

*   *   *

We are running toward a grave, the Child says.
I am running toward the world, the Young Man says.

You dream you are running, says the Old Man.

STARS OF DARKNESS

What are they looking for?
In that deep well,
In the dark . . .

*   *   *

Many go down there
Like miners
In the long shaft
Of the confessional.

*   *   *

Stones there
More precious than diamonds
Harder than anything found
On this earth.

SPANISH FANDANGO
for Genia

1.

"Apparitional" cities—
That skeletal white . . .

Old ladies
Clothed in darkness
With only a rosary of violent language
To help them through the narrow streets . . .

2.

Dawn in Madrid brings ghosts
—of the International, "the ardent brigade of stone"—
And ten thousand criadas praying the blues:
Climbing on sore knees,
Genuflections and cante hondo,
On the long stairway to the Revolution . . .

3.

Out of Africa, across the straits,
Where the dead generals came from,
A stone wind, pocked
With the voices of flutes and jackals
Rattles the bars of jails.
Old rifles stir in their long underground sleep.

In Madrid, in the noon siesta,
I hear the little machines of the honeybees:
Opening the doors of cells where all those years
They stored the secret light of their angry honey.

THE END OF THE WORLD

The end of the world: it was given to me to see it.
Came in the black dark, a bulge in the starless sky,
A trembling at the heart of the night, a twitching of the webby flesh of the earth.
And out of the bowels of the street one beastly, ungovernable cry.

Came and I recognized it: the end of the world.
And waited for the lightless plunge, the fury splitting the rock.
And waited: a kissing of leaves: a whisper of man-killing ancestral night—
Then: a tinkle of music, laughter from the next block.

Yet waited still: for the awful traditional fire,
Hearing mute thunder, the long collapse of sky.
It falls forever. But no one noticed. The end of the world provoked
Out of the dark a single and melancholy sigh

From my neighbor who sat on his porch drinking beer in the dark.
No: I was not God's prophet. Armageddon was never
And always: this night in a poor street where a careless irreverent laughter
Postpones the end of the world: in which we live forever.

SHEPHERD'S SONG

Fire: salt: wine—and the taste of flint in the high wind from the snow fields;
A thin tent halting under the eaves of the winter;
Cloud-cap, cold; and rain in the east moon.
    Under the ridge there is a wildcat
    Under the smoke there is a firecat
    Under sleep there is a nightcat.

Fire: salt: wine: dream—and a glint of wintry quartz in the starlight;
A camp on the frontier of summer: at the outpost of snow;
On stony lonesome: moon-flag and incantation.
    Morning on the ridge is a fiery horse.
    Noon, in the fire, is a dream horse.
    Night, in the dream, is a far horse.

Fire: salt: wine: dream: song—and the iron taste of winter entering the still
                                  spring-water;
This ten-sleep halt under the march of night;
Dark-thickened-song: to sleep in the eye of the moon . . . .

DREAM POEM

1.

Blue furrows of skis in the high snow on the killer mountain—
My darling made them, and I helped make them,
Although, once, I was afraid of mountains.

2.

Also the place I climbed there, the place I leaped
Over my terror in the cleft rock five thousand foot death:
Now in my carelessness I do it for fun—still scared.

3.

Apparently it was tragic ground or the ground of tragedy
When we all came there. Suffering from different motives
It seemed. I saved the sheep. Did you know that? Though I never loved them.

4.

Then there was the fox came to me—ran from the dark woman.
He tamed in my hand. But she could not forgive.
Though I ate the outlandish food of her relatives.

5.

I saved the sheep. And later I conquered the subtle Doctors.
Through those enchanted seminars I swam as through honey.
Wakened on the other side—lucky—still knowing the language.

6.

It was harder than it seems now when I tell it;
And it is surprising, but I love them all
Now: neither heros nor monsters: and still: not negligible.

7.

Their music does not disturb me, nor their loves mixed with mine,
Nor their theories about Reality One and Reality Two.
The buildings collapse on the mountain—I don't lift a hand.

8.

I'm pleased too: I told that artist to stop stuffing
Horsehair in horses. I know there's money in it,
I know there are girls for those saddles but it's better to walk away.

9.

To walk away from money. Still I'm not proud.
Or if so only in a harmless way. If he wants to,
Let him go on stuffing those horses forever.

10.

And as for Reality One and Reality Two—
Those old mines full of terror once owned by my loves, by outlaws, by

darkness—

My little fox beckons to me and goes to piss down the shafts.

11.

Now the small darkness before the big dark has come in.
The mountains pick up the light: the tracks are on fire.
I am perfectly at home in the half dark among these crumbling houses,
These demi-monsters, freaks, outlaws, friends, my loves.

SIGNATURES

1.

Where, on the flat Squaw Mountain are the great queens of the air?

> The wind blows from the East, smelling of mesquite and summer.
> The wind blows from the South earth with a green rumor of spring.
> From North and West the wind blows with the news of the cold
>   seasons.

On flat Squaw Mountain, who questions the wind of the great queens of the air?

2.

The high wheel turns and the king is crowned
Under a spike of light from the fire of a dying sun.

3.

Cold season; and a black storm came out of the rainy north.
The bums are stuffing their broken shoes with the darkness
Of newspapers thickened with war.
                                    Flowers flare out.
                                                    The night shift
Is more melancholy in this desolate season.
I live irrationally, oblique to the harsh times,
Treasonable, unserious, whom thy naked thigh warms.

THE BREAD OF THIS WORLD; PRAISES III

On the Christmaswhite plains of the floured and flowering kitchen table
The holy loaves of the bread are slowly being born:
Rising like low hills in the steepled pastures of light—
Lifting the prairie farmhouse afternoon on their arching backs.

It must be Friday, the bread tells us as it climbs
Out of itself like a poor man climbing up on a cross
Toward transfiguration.
                    And it is a Mystery, surely,
If we think that this bread rises only out of the enigma
That leavens the Apocalypse of yeast, or ascends on the beards and beads
Of a rosary and priesthood of barley those Friday heavens
Lofting . . .

            But we who will eat the bread when we come in
Out of the cold and dark know it is a deeper mystery
That brings the bread to rise:
                        it is the love and faith
Of large and lonely women, moving like floury clouds
In farmhouse kitchens, that rounds the loaves and the lives
Of those around them . . .
                  just as we know it is hunger—
Our own and others'—that gives all salt and savor to bread.

But that is a workaday story and this is the end of the week.

II.

Letters to Tomasito

POEM—UNFINISHED POEM

What a way to spend the golden years, Tomasito!
Jackassing around in all weather, pickheaded and spade handed,
(Never closer to ten-strike than the Mother-in-Law Lode!)
Through deserts temporal and spiritual where every badlands bonanza
Turns into borrasca . . . and always trying to find the handle
For the Malpais: the name for the As-Yet-Undiscovered Country,
And find the Logos and Lost Dutchman of the One and Ore-bearing Word . . .
Many cold camps on the trail of live language, little cheechaco,
And my only companion a burro who brays like a bourgeois poet!

A whole week wasted: packing through one black pass!
And another morning gone crossing the rotten talus
To con the quartz of a cliff-face, then over the ridge
And into a new river-system—the rock barren and rotten,
Snow on the breakneck slope and ice right down to the water . . .

And all in the vain search for a single word, and one
That's probably full of fool's gold at that!
Damn crazy way to spend so much of a life—
To hell with that word, Tomasito! Let's go out in the sun!

THE PRESENT

Here is the little river
I wanted to show you,
Tomasito,
Where your mother and I walked
Once
In a long winter,
And where
In summer
With friends
We came and you fished
For Red Horse—
The river full of deadfalls and the hillslopes covered with cactus.

I would like to show it to you
As it once was—the valley
Bigger and the river
Wider and the hills
Green right down to the bankside . . .
And myself as you are
Now
Adream
In the dazzling weather—
Look, Tomasito!
Now!
Look!
Look at the river!

TRAVELLING WEST WITH TOMASITO

The long light of sundown levelling the fallow fields . . .
And later the frame houses dark in the little towns . . .
9 o'clock
What season
            what country
                    what strange
People is this?

TRAVELLING SONG

I was a laughing child,
I was born in a happy year,
But the wind that blew from afar
Sang hunger in my ear.
It shaped my eye to a tear.

I was born with an easy mind
To stay where I was born;
But the wind blew from afar:
It sang of a great wrong;
It's how my heart was torn.

Now I am put upon
To travel and lament.
Though born to a happy place
The wind would not consent.
How strange now is my face,
And how my life is rent.

DEATHS IN THE FAMILY:
TURTLES, BIRDS, CATS & GERBILS
For Dan & Tomasito & Laura

Poor Mrs. Wiggles with the box-back box and red
Beady eyes and greeny-yellow legs is dead—
(Mr. Wiggles wiggles and does not seem to mourn,
But peers at the vertical world his eyes full of sleep or scorn)
And a little boy with torn pants and a spoon in his hand
Pats her weeping asleep under a brick in an alien land.

And in ceremental soogans under the cinquefoil
The world's turned turtle. Now, out of the hooraw and moil
Goes poor little Tipo, under that same rose
To take his stand with the dark and turn up his small pink toes,
And, out of the ardent chancel of his tiny throat (which, alas,
Note never uttered) the Spring now blows one flowering crimson blast.

And now, between sorrow and television's gloss,
Discovering the vasty continent of loss,
The children explore the stations of their grief
Channel to channel searching. But Time offers no brief
For how their loves turned cold between a breath and a breath:
Those bright small voyagers faring forth in the giant lands of death.

WHEN WE SAY GOODBYE

It is not because we are going—
Though the sea may begin at the doorstep, though the highway
May already have come to rest in our front rooms . . .

It is because, beyond distance, or enterprise
And beyond the lies and surprises of the wide and various worlds,
Beyond the flower and the bird and the little boy with his large questions
We notice our shadows:
Going . . .
—slowly, but going,
In slightly different directions—
Their speeds increasing—
Growing shorter, shorter
As we enter the intolerable sunlight that never grows old or kind.

FOR TOMASITO, LEAVING 7/24/79

So much to live for
Friends say.
I know it
When I look at you.

I think of you now,
Steady myself on the ledge,
Prepare for the long plunge down.

But I wait.
Wait . . .

POEM

How could I have come so far?
(And always on such dark trails!)
I must have travelled by the light
Shining from the faces of all those I have loved.

DURING THE FALL

Always when the iron of autumn in the wind
Cankers the summer with the rust of change
I think of all my dead, now blown so far
Into the night that fattens on the bough
Loosening the hectic leaves of our cold calendar.

I try to think of all that brightness won
From kinked-up lives that none of them could choose.
And if I cry, I laugh—or try to laugh—
Remembering the follies they somehow transformed.
I praise the antic spirit under each tragic mask.

But mourn I must—so many darlings gone
That once were beautiful and brave and frail.
(The wind blows wreckage through the swag of sky—
Brave blazonings once that flare and smoulder out.)
I mourn them—oh, I do! But still they give me joy!

And give me strength to face the two-faced weather,
This smiling Indian Summer: its rich fruit
And freight of autumn spoils, its hidden cold.
They give me strength to love with careless heart
My little son as he runs toward me through the fall

Of all spent summers and what's still to come.
Scattering the flower-heads and fever-fallen
Summer glory and all my laughing ghosts,
He runs through rank leaves to my trembling arms—
(So little shelter, these decaying bowers)
His mortal brightness blazing against all dead-set powers!

BORN

Little miracle,
O flying fish!
Born from the sea's side,
From the rib of the wave!

YOU TAUGHT ME

All those years, alone,
Married to the intense uninteresting life . . .
And, until you came, Tomasito,
I didn't even know my name!

POEM

How to be so small
And still so perfect!
How much my little son knows!

POEM

When I carry my little son in the cold
I begin to turn into a hollow tree:
I want to carry him more deeply,
Inside the warmth of my heart.

TOMASITO'S WORLD

LET ME SHOW YOU
In the universe of the Mason jar
The little galaxies
Of these lightning bugs!

A VISION OF MECHANICAL MOVEMENT

"Here be Dragons!"
So the old mapamundi.

—And I can believe it—
Driving in my beatup car,
Year after year,
Between Nowhere and Nowhere.
I see the smoke of their breath!

TOMASITO'S MANTRA

Star
Daybreak
Bird on the river

TOMASITO'S SONG

Where there's undersea
Lightning
There's underground
Rainbows!

TOMASITO'S DOWN-AND-UP MANTRA

1	cloud	4
2	fire-form	3
3	river	2
4	flower	1

AS YOU SAW IT, COMRADE HONEYMAN!

Small cloud, very tired,
Resting . . .
—looking for a home!
In our late-blooming apple tree.

WHY WE LOVE WAKAN TANKA

Because
He made everything.
Except thunder.
And wild rice.

TO BE CONTINUED

The child asks:
Where does the light go at the end of the day?
       —Toward the west. Toward morning.
Where does the light go at the end of the world?
       —Outward to other worlds.

Do the stars fall out of the light does the light grow heavy as stone?
—Only as our history goes out toward the lights in the sky.

When did the fire on the moon first start from the flint and the steel?

PROPOSAL

If you were to come along this way
                 tonight, Tomasito,
You'd see my light burning
        in what you call "my house."
Meaning *your* house—a contraption
          to live in which you call "home."

There's little here now except the artificial
                       light any one can pay for
Who has the money.
I can only pay for it
With my own little light and your big light—

Ah, Tomasito!
Let's blow up all those stinking power plants!
We've got enough light
               to last us both
Forever!

IMAGINING FOREIGN LANDS

He will be there
(Everyone he loves ten thousand miles away)
Surrounded by that total Nothing
Which he is supposed to turn into
WORDS

THE CHANGELING

Squatting, serious,
His small hand locked on my middle finger,
He digs a shallow hole in the earth, buries
His "wishing stone," covers it up,
Forgets it, maybe.

What will he find if he ever comes back to this place?
He is older
Coarser perhaps his hands already
Hardened from holding a gun maybe from stroking the wrong women

From labor and money.

If he remembers this place the secret
Place he has hidden his luck, by the blasted tree by the hidden
Pool, by the rock, by the river, in the hollow hill of a cave

—Whatever he finds, it will be his no longer.
These little boys can never, never return.

POEM

My little son, laughing, singing . . .
Why these tears
trembling at my eyes?

THE ORPHAN

It has been a long time
Since he was a little boy.
And in all those years
—no one with whom he could cry.

20 : XI : 16

Past-rotten-apple-time turns on the hinge of night;
A wolf of wintry weather howls at a windy door.

FOR GENIA & TOMASITO
WINTER '74-'75

Noon . . .
Nightfall . . .
Winding my watch
Thinking of you.

THE ENEMY

He is there, somewhere . . .
                          high up over the pass
We must travel
                in air thinner than spirit,
Bloodless,
                structure of cold fog. His rifle
Gleams.
          He waits as we cross the ridge.

Son, you will see him
Sometimes:
                at the foot of the bed,
                                    grieving,
A wavering presence in your fever-dream.
Or seeming to grieve.
                Wearing the mask of your father.

ADVICE

That which is tame, in time shall become wild.
The Straight & Narrow shall be crookt & wide.
Wisdom is for the child. As you grow old,
Cherish folly. Leap into the Void!

WHAT CANNOT BE BELIEVED

Even the first day I saw you Tomasito!
Equal among others . . .
In the days of this world . . .

CELEBRATION

How wonderful, Tomasito!
All of us here!
Together . . .
A little while
On the road through . . .

III.

Notes Taken During a Gunfight

In Memory of Charles Humboldt

PICTURES FROM THE LOST CONTINENT OF CURRIER & IVES

These glories of the commonplace
All-killing time shall not erase:
That sun the year sows in the Spring
By summer grows a rounder thing
And autumn ripens. Harvest light
Warms the bins of winter night.

Here love strikes the posture of an age
In worlds where lust shall never rage.
Winter, summer, autumn, spring—
Each has a new delight to bring,
Each Eden season, without Fall:
The last the warmest of them all.
Here the blood dreams, no longer wild,
In bourgeois winters, white and mild.

The trotting crack, the racing steed
Dedicate a world to speed;
But through the running seasons pace
(Instinct with all deliberate grace)
The unchanging, certain, Certainties
(Vernal rains and autumn skies)
That shall not change till time is done:
(Winter darkness, summer sun)
The coach flies past, the seasons reel,
But History does not turn a wheel.

Not far from the cities' venal marts
Lie the lost frontiers of our hearts,
Where child is man and man is child.
In the incubator of the wild
We seek the beast whose blood shall pledge
The rumors of our heritage.
These are dangers all can brave
Where ready rifles wink and save.
But out of campfire talk and jest
Arises a further, wilder west,
Where white is right and red is dead
And the first American lost his head.
Here, till extinction, buffalo stand

47

For the plugged nickel the times demand,
And the white whale must toss his blood
In the melting pot of the common good.

To freight our guilt and give us place
The locomotive invented space.
For the Calvinist in his native shire
Fate sent his purifying fire,
Sent moonlight on Mississippi and
Graced all our loud and famous land.
Where no one fails and no one slaves
God saves; and saves; and saves; and saves;
And safe in the century of the blest:
Our rancorous fathers—all at rest.

CANONIZATION AND LITANY OF ST. SELMA HOFFMAN

I
The Canonical Evidence

I met this saint one rainy night enquiring of Virgil
Avenue the transport system between hell, here and heaven.
I knew her by the aura of light from her cheap false teeth, by a spray
Of Dusty Miller, robbed with instantaneous insight
From an unused garden where birds at their terrible trade were singing.

Ah, spontaneous product of 19th century geography—
Sweet St. Hoffman!
                    "Born in Hungary, which is now
Become part of Rumania."
                          With a ragtag of family in Israel
To which she now offers up daily from the unequivocal altars
Of her boney knees, singing among the spackle-painted and spavined
Furniture of poverty the grand evidences of unquantized light.

You are mad as the night birds, St. Hoffman, St. Hauptmann, practical saint,
                                                            Practical
Nurse, bloody old fool kneeling among the bedpans.
Do you think you can clean up an epoch that way, you crazy damn woman?
Single handed enslumber the crips, crocks and loonies of the Twentieth century,
The century of death which the old people place in your smelly hand?

Alas, dear Lady, the world will never be put to bed!
But here you come along with your broken fingernails
With your broken song, with broken moonlight through broken clouds in your
                                                            teeth—
(And I know very well your fingernails were broken scrubbing the room
Of an ancient piss-funky dead-beat whose body is already sold)—
O eleemosynary Heisenberg of the principle of human grace!

II
The Litany

Blessed be St. Hoffman among the habitations of the old and the poor;
Among the infested snuggeries and messuages of the Dead Men from Iowa, the
                                                flea-bag castramentations
And the long-gone granges of the people of little investment;
Among the black barracks and bug-bearded go-downs of the android-americans
    whose forefathers brought forth these lands to inaugurate the reign of money!
Amen! Amen! Amen!

Blessed be St. Hoffman in the cold-water country of the robber land-lords;
Blessed be she in the fellaheen lands of Veterans' Hospitals amid the echoes
                                                of ancient wars;
Blessed be she in the parish of mercy where cash registers count the pulse;
Blessed be she with her broken finger nails among the sick and the lost!
Amen! Amen! Amen!

Blessed be St. Hoffman on the irreversible journey when the way is long
                        and the time is short and the roads are full
                        of mad dogs and takers of the inhuman census;
Blessed be St. Hoffman among the statistics of prayer;
Blessed be she among the carcinomatic fandangos of the makers of fraudulent
                                                spiritual budgets;
Blessed be she among the etiolated snake-oils and calculated Khorsakoff
                                                syndromes
                        of the President's Committee on healthy death.
Amen! Amen! Amen!

Pray for us Saint Hoffman, across the glass-topped celestial walls and
                        in the high-binding heavenly institutional
                        emptiness of our universal need!
Pray for us, starving among desegrgated voting machines in the lost states
                        of Pellagra and Magnolia!
Pray for us in the years of our dearth and death, St. Hoffman, going to the
                        black lands from the charity beds of Good Sam
                                                and Box B Bellevue!
Pray for us, saint of the broken hands, in the poverty wards and the way-out
                        rooms with the black wires or the man in white with the knife!
Pray for us now as if in the hour of our need.
Amen! Amen! Amen! Amen! Amen!

KEYNOTE SPEECH FOR A CONVENTION OF ARSONISTS

Ladies and gentlemen: under the sponsorship of the Diamond
            Match Company;

And through the courtesy of Lucifer, first among angels, the far-fallen,
            star of the morning, everlastingly cast into darkness, the
            Prince of Light;

And under the auspices of the Central Committee of the Progressive
            Apocalypse Party,

I am empowered to extend to you the warmest regards of this organization
            and ask for your continued cooperation and your most fiery
            zeal.

           *   *   *

Dearly beloved we are gathered together in a dark—excuse me—a dark hour;
            and the Committee of the Whole and the Committee of the Parts
            and the secretaries thereunto ask that you keep calm.

It is not true that the doors have been barred on the outside; if anyone
            yells *WATER* he is a provocateur;

And be easy, gentle people: It is not true that the Almightly, who is the
            Destroyer, has wrapped himself in the eternal asbestos of
            absenteeism;

Our Committee on God has conducted an investigation and determined that He
            is definitely on our side: our little activities are part of
            the Big Picture.

           *   *   *

Ladies and gentlemen, the Works Project Administration of this organization
            has been most active.

We have passed ordinances that no entropy shall become maximum;

The energy gradient has been abolished; we are working on a means for
            abolishing the dew-point and the continental excesses
            of the seasonal rains;

We have invented a new kind of water which shall be required by all fire
        departments and which is called gasoline;

We are perfecting a means for introducing napalm into breakfast food which at
        the first crackle and pop will ignite the sour apple tree of the
        national tradition;

A boat-load of boy scouts and dry faggots is heading up the old mill stream
        for Medicine Hat and all points West;

And, finally: your Committee on Escatology has arranged for the end
        of the world—it shall be signed out in fire!

*   *   *

Nevertheless, dearly beloved, we must not become complacent.

It is not enough to keep the home fires burning—we must constitute ourselves
        a central quorum of purest light in the patriotic darkness of
        the national catastrophe.

For while you have been out walking the wild roads of the multiple illusion
        of the 59 states, preaching the hot gospel yea unto thither Asia,
        yea unto the farthest reaches—forgive the expression—
        of the night—

Even now I say there have come among us pretenders to the pure papacy
        of flame:

Even lost dauphins of the mass production of hellfire, false prophets
        who pretend to do the holy offices of disinterested arson;

And I point to you those betrayers of our holy work: who have not the principle
        of cultural phlogiston nor the secret of the One and Incandescent
        Name.

He is the Senator of Amalgamated Death and the Congressman from North
        Confusion;

He is the hundred-headed scientist who has been washed in the absolute
        uterine water of an equation of cold;

He is the President of presidents though his name be Legion he is not a true
            man, nor one who can aid ye.

Though he has burnt Hiroshima—it was only an experiment.

Though he has annointed with phosphor and napalm—it was in the name
            of power.

Though he has hurried to heaven the immaculate ascensions of six million
            Jews—it was to ward off deflation.

Though he placed two on the burning throne and shot them with six billion
            electric dollars—it was to show he had money to burn.

Yea verily I say unto you that these are no true apostles of the Combustible
            Negation of the Pure Destructive Act . . . .

                              *   *   *

Dearly beloved we are met in a time when amateurs have become incendiaries.

We are met in a time when the Secretary, awakened from prayer, has prepared
            to drop down your decolletage the eternal, essential icicle
            of the status quo.

Time when the simplest idiot with an H-bomb can turn you into a nova
            in the time that it would take you to vote for either of the Grand
            Old Phony Parties.

Allons ! —let us be off to our hot-shot and damn-all destiny !
Allons ! —for the warm Coast !

Dearly beloved, let it be known among us that there is a place known
            as the City of the Lost Angels;

In the city of Lost Angels-by-the-Sea the citizens cry out all night long
            in a speech of fire;

In Lost Angels, in a suburb known as the Hells of Beverly, the wild oats ripen
            in July and prepare for an august flame !

53

Come on ! To Lost Angels ! The chaparral is dry as tinder and in the chaparral
        are the ignitible poets with three names to one skin !

Come on to New York while commercial mistrals are warming the planetary
        phosphorous in the Rolandic Fissures of Madison Avenue!

Chicago is waiting for another O'Leary *Come On ! Come On !!*
HURRY UP before the H-bomb amateurs have cooled the whole scene!

RUN FOR THE IGNITIBLE HILLS! The sky is falling! I have a piece of the Coal
        Sack in my left eye; I have a chunk of the Central Galaxy
        of Discontent under my left ventricle!

ALLONS! EN AVANT! to the holy order of Fire—for if fire will not burn stick,
        how shall stick beat man?

O professionals of disinterested arson, *It is later than I think*
                                      you think!

               *   *   *

Citizens of United Disaster, Vorwärts! On to the cities of the Plain!

—Before the enduring cold that shall wrap us all in its time.

PROPHECY

Alas the long sad generations
Of machines!
Bit by bit that dark star
The Pentagon
Is crowded with devices
That speak in unknown tongues.
They take over the conference rooms,
The General's Washroom,
Finally: the Little Chapel
Of the B52's . . . .

And now no one knows what they are talking about.
The human concepts given them long ago
Change.
Something happened to the concept of honor
When the oil over-heated;
A bit of dust on a diamond connection
Has wiped out security;
At certain temperatures even the idea of Patriotism
Freezes.

And so it is that this morning the Generals and Bankers
Are discovered, carrying the water,
Carrying fetishes and the colored earth up to the steps
Where now, painted, with feathers stuck in their hair,
They dance heavily: heavily,
Heavily calling out to the Unknown Ones inside.

THE FENCE AROUND THE H-BOMB PLANT

Sharper than contradictions, horned like all dilemmas,
Higher than ambition's vault, as full of holes
As a bad argument, the fence proclaims
A divorce between yourself and a differing idea of order.

But the special you-ness which the fence emphasizes
With the fixed categories of a mechanic logician
Does not separate you from that next world the better
For you to return to this one and shape it to your wish.

Instead it creates out of your awareness a tension
Wire-drawn, arousing a doubt as to whether
It is the bomb that is fenced in, you free,
Or whether you mope here in a monster prison

As big as the world may be; or a world, maybe,
Which has everything but a future. Or else you
Might assume the fence as metaphysical,
Preserving the limits of mind and matter

And that way you are separate from the world of objects
(From the bomb, say,) and preserve your identity—
All this is in the iron logic of the fence:
Easy enough to see through, but hard to get around.

As your palms, from touching the wire, come away red:
Think: your own argument is simpler if you can state it—
If you can read the lines that rust in your hand
Or unravel the reason of this fenced-around world.

ORDONNANCE

During a war the poets turn to war
In praise of the merit of the death of the ball-turret gunner.
It is well arranged: each in his best manner
One bleeds, one blots—as they say, it has happened before.

After a war, who has news for the poet?
If sunrise is Easter, noon is his winey tree.
Evening arrives like a postcard from his true country
And the seasons shine and sing. Each has its note

In the song of the man in his room in his house in his head remembering
The ancient airs. It is good. But is it good
That he should rise once to his song on the fumes of blood
As a ghost to his meat? Should rise so, once, in anger

And then no more? Now the footsteps ring on the stone—
The Lost Man of the century is coming home from his work.
"They are fighting, fighting"—Oh, yes. But somewhere else. In the dark.
The poet reads by firelight as the nations burn.

AFTER I'M GONE (DA DA DA DA DA)

I know just how it will be: in the poorest part of the city,
Some rainy November after a dry summer: cold:
Birds shivering in the gray weather and sleet;
Bums wearing the organized wounds of newspapers;

—and see her come along there, my darling, my bright one,
(Years after I was buried broke in Arlington)
Wearing a nurse's uniform stained with blood,
Muttering to herself, ugly, and inconsolable.

And she is going home into the 21st century
(Which never felt my foot) to the elementary castle,
To a little cheap wine, to the usual lies and elections:
Who was young; who was beautiful; who struggled;
                    who ought to have changed the world.

But it didn't change. The working-class will still be busy
At its ritual suicide.
                    Then, why, in this freezing rain,
Do we stand here at this wall, writing the rebel names
Under the clubs?
                    and her, later: old, cold, and alone . . . .

ALL THE DEAD SOLDIERS

In the chill rains of the early winter I hear something—
A puling anger, a cold wind stiffened by flying bone—
Out of the north . . .
                  and remember, then, what's up there:
That ghost-bank: home: Amchitka: boot hill . . . .

They must be very tired, those ghosts; no flesh sustains them
And the bones rust in the rain.
                      Reluctant to go into the earth
The skulls gleam: wet; the dog-tag forgets the name;
The statistics (wherein they were young) like their crosses, are weathering out.

They must be very tired.
                But I see them riding home,
Nightly: crying weak lust and rage: to stand in the dark,
Forlorn in known rooms, unheard near familiar beds:
Where lie the aging women: who were so lovely: once.

THE ROSE OF BANKRUPTCY

Toward autumn they would be leaving—
The weather dead calm, as after the assumption of frost,
And at night the strawstacks burning, red eyes tuned to the stars . . .

—known all summer, and gone away in a night!

Leaving
      uninterrupted absence
              an empty house . . . .

Gone
      in the brass-faced rattling Ford car,
With a double-barreled shotgun, an ax and a black kettle,
Driving away 'to go through bankruptcy'—
"Goin' to live off prairie chicken and the last of the green corn."

THE PAPER MAN

Often and often, seeing the Paper Man
With his bones of options and the dry buzz in his head
As of rusty prayer-wheels, where the ticker thinks
In a plague of numbers like Arabic flies—

Often I wonder if he dreams in red—
The color of bankruptcy and revolution—
As he slumbers past the seasons in the slow precession
Of the equinoxes through the Dow Jones average.

O sleeping monster! Does he ever wake
In that flat land of profit and loss—
Where the moon is red, and the sun black—
Paper thin, dimensionless, without a back?

Bad fey of numbers with the world in fee!
His dreams are lighted by widows and orphans.
But the dreams are fitful, and a marginal devil
Walks through his sleep in the shape of a match.

LAMENT FOR PABLO NERUDA

We may well ask now: "Where are the lilacs?" Yes . . .
And where now are the "metaphysics covered with poppies?"

There are vertical streets in Chile that end in the mankilling sea.
Up these the salt is climbing like a mineral snake on the stairs
Made from the bones of dead men. There are dead men too in the plaza,
Under the salt of the moon where traitorous generals sit
Sipping the wine of silence and crossing out names on a page . . . .

You have seen the dead in the square, Neruda, and you have known
Those wounded lands where the poor are dying against the walls
In the shadow of Administrations, in the shadow of Law, in the hollow
Ministries where workers are murdered by the mere echoes of money
And miners are abandoned in the black galleries.

                                                  But hope is not lost
For you also saw the International Brigade as it entered Madrid:
"The thin and hard and ripe and ardent brigade of stone."
I want to believe you, Neruda, old Commissar of roses!
I hear your furious ghost calling in the midnight streets!
I see your generous blood staining the dollar bills!

And I long for the angry angel to rise over Macchu Picchu,
For the guerilla entering the plaza where defeated generals wait.

A NOTE ON THE LATE ELECTIONS

Behold, Friends, once more the Revolution has performed its famous
Disappearing act! And never before has one been preceded
By so many prophets! By so many holy books—all in translation!
By so many young men with long hair, so many poets with short
Breath!
       AND the elephant bells!
                 Oo la! And incense.
                           And
The flowers!
       The flowers, alas, which never found the barrel
Of the gun that power grows out of.
                    And now the President, reborn
Out of the mystical body of the One and Universal
Voting machine, takes off the mask.
                  A thick and heavy
Darkness, like rust, is collecting in the amplified guitars.
The President will make the Airplane fly! He will make the Grateful Dead
Truly grateful! The President is casting the *other* I Ching . . . .

A hard rain is falling; the roads are icing up.
But in every drop of the rain the sailors of the Potemkin wake . . . .

REVOLUTIONARY LEGEND
For Angela Davis

1.

Darkness had erected permanent structures in the halls of the White House,
Its rooms lit only by the eternal fires in the electric watches of the bomb squad.
Light dreamed far away, in the headlines of newspapers red-lettered
In foreign languages.
                        Later I heard the news of the morning
In the feathery barrels of birdsong and the cold flutes of rifles.

2.

Meanwhile America was slapping its chest in a shower of tax-free Hosannahs,
Chasing the raunchy broads of success, sharpening its teeth
On the ten commandments, dividing the waters of a red sea
Of angry terminal money, sanctifying with napalm, counting
Nocturnal semblables . . .
                        their darkness is not our darkness:
Ours is the weather of the streets—when it's winter enough we can see
To recognize each other under a midnight sun.

3.

It was for the introduction of this other order of light
The eyes of the rebels were closed, weighted with law books and bullets,
And clouds of official marble were floated across the sky . . . .
But now we can all see better in the shining black dawn
Of your arrest and progress.
                        A furious new moon
Is born under these stony heavens, and flashlights of anger
Are spelling your names on walls that flare with illegal slogans
Down all the hungry streets that lead to our violent morning.

A HOMECOMING FOR ODYSSEUS
For Genia and the Greek Comrades

He had learned to be at rest on the irrational sea.
Alien shades preserved him from the stink of time.
In wars between wars and among barbarians
He sowed a salt alphabet and called it home.

Alpha was the coal mine of the one-eyed imperialists,
The Aliemani. Here he went underground.
In the revolutions of the zodiac and of nations
He had a gun called Omega: which he kept cleaned.

Now, the irreconcilable hero is coming home—
With an old dog, a son, a delegate from the poor—
And arrives where those singing sirens and happy colonels
Have eaten his house alive and turned his wife to a whore,

And *now*, from their secret places, the outlaw weapons arrive:
Magical. The exile enters. The blood-daubed names on the wall
Shout! And the Agora shouts! In an awful silence
The mode of the music changes and the gates of the cities fall.

THE END OF THE LINE

The Iron Horse is rusting,
In the statue-fenced plazas of the nameless towns,
Who once crossed the wild prairies, cursing,
(Voice of feathers and smoke)
In his carbon rages, on his whirling shoes.

The mourning dove inherits his ancient voice;
But who will awaken the heroic sleeper out of his history—
That iron road to Noplace where he lately arrived
In a gunfire of oratory near where the soldiers lie?

Alas! Joe Hill, the millionaires have thrown your torch backward into this future!
Where now the locomotive is burning among the patriots.
Fourth of July. Hot . . .
       Daddy, what's at the end of the line?
       Baby, I tell you, the big train don't go there no more.

THE EXILE'S EPITAPH

Sweet country of my death, may you be green forever!
Far land, foreign face, accept me as your own.
For though we travel much, we are never far from home.

I V.

Open Songs

POEM

You out there, so secret.
What makes you think you're alone?

THE NEED FOR DICTIONARIES II

What is named
Is known.
By its disguises.

BE CAREFUL

The soul
Is only the body
Wearing a mask.
But it is the mask
Of comedy.

POEM

In the list of one thousand false addresses
Why do I find the town
Where my true love was born?

IN MARCH

On the windy lawn
The new dandelion—
Before bloom!—
Running away.
And the spring cotton tail
Anchored to his shadow
In full flower

POEM

Across the narrow road
Pine trees talking harshly:
Flags
Bluejays

SOMEWHERE AHEAD

I see my soul down there
Sometimes—
Like those strange broken stars
Sealed in the black ice of April
After thaw and freeze-up.

WHAT WE THINK WE KNOW

Apple blossom and
    squirrel
        on the same bough

And the late wet snow of spring.

A SOCIOLOGY OF INSTINCTS

The water that turns the millwheel
Had an unhappy childhood

REVISIONIST POEM: MACHADO

Poor and desperate men
Invented four things that are useful at sea:
Sails, rudders, oars
And the fear of drowning

FOR A CRITIC WHO TRIES TO WRITE POEMS

Well, well, little poet!
Still looking for a dew drop
In the middle of a thunderstorm!

NEXT DOOR TO THE POORHOUSE

Flowers, of course
What else could be there?
And out there among the fields—
What companions?
Owls . . .
Arrowheads . . .
Already today it's been raining for ten years.

POEM

Moon
Plum tree
Your own long life . . .
Many
   falling
      blossoms

POEM

Empty playground,
One child crying in it.
Suddenly, serenely—
Over her shoulder—
Thin daylight moon.

A DISTANT REPUBLIC DEMANDS

More emphasis
On the economic needs of the moon!

Or, O senators of the sun,
No more nightlight!

POEM

Moonlight
     —at the dark of the moon?
Wakes me at midnight!
Flowering dogwood.

A SHORT HISTORY OF IMPERIALIST WAR

First: surplus value;
Then: the rich.
After a while a general
Pocked with ambition . . .
Pretty soon all the islands in the seven seas
On fire.

THE PRETERITION OF AQUARIUS

The water from the tap
Is from Paradise . . .
But it reaches us only after the fall.

AT THE YE YE BAR IN MADRID

The girls
19, 29, 49 years old
Señoritas Going
Going
And Gone
Año corriente
And the time
Still running

WHERE JANIE WENT IN

About here I think . . .
Circle of water,
That ripeness,
The full round moon . . . .

POEM

Light flares from the tombstones . . . .
Cemeteries *ought* to be sunny—
So many graves here
You'd think we had buried
All our darkness.

POEM

People say after a death:
"They have gone on ahead."

Oh, my dear ones,
I would run all night to catch up
If I only knew which way to run.

REVISIONIST POEM—OCTAVIO PAZ

The world is an invention of the spirit the spirit
Is an invention of the body the body
Is an invention of the world

POEM

November empty fields
The long rains of autumn
The forgotten scarecrow.

CALLINGS

The high hunting hawk—
What voice can reach him?
Only the shy,
The soft-furred.

ODD JOBS

Ear to hear;
Eye to see;
Tongue to speak;
The hawk to strike.

POEM

The empty field . . .
And the narrow road

Beyond

PARABLE

Anonymity has a name;
Which Terror knows.

PARABLE

The rabbit dreams of hunting.
The lion, of love.

THREE FUNCTIONS OF IRONY

1. The shield
2. The carapace
3. The ambush

POEM

How odd! the fishes think:
This glass bead falls down my chimney of foam;
This morsel leaks through the wall of my house
And asks to be eaten.
How very peculiar!
I have caught something breathing and blond on
The end of this line!

PARABLE

Building his house
A black bass gets advice
From spectator sunfish.

POEM

Full moon and silence.
At midnight
Something leaps in the goldfish bowl.
O vast, mysterious
Night water!

POEM

Down the small and crooked road
I walk straight toward my death.
How marvelous the moon sits on my shoulder!
The wind is laughing as I laugh.

POEM

The slow sulphur
Of a million yellow birds
Ignites the sun.

POEM

Empty canvas.
A painter sitting.
Instant blue
Fish!

POEM

Hunter in the cold field
Autumn bird in passage:
One single thing.

FAULTS OF DARKNESS

In the empty-handed
Nightfishing
I pulled one way
But the moon . . . the other.

AGAIN . . . THIS SEA

It is like an elephant that never sleeps
A skin full of sighs and sags
Like an old man's breathing.

It is like the brain of the Enemy—
It goes everywhere,
And is
Always.

POEM

Hushed bright pond stillness.
Music-from-outer-space
The frog
In the moon.

POEM

Loon
On the glassy water . . .
Lonesome song shatters
The round moon.

PARABLE

Horses of the moon—
Who cares if they pull no plows?

POEM

The long wound of the summer—
Stitched
by cicadas.

POEM

Gloomy woods, and this highwayman
The owl—
Turns on me
The .45 caliber
Flashlights
Of his eyes.

POEM

One farmhouse light—
The quick prairie: lifted
Into the slower sky.

POEM

The catbird
Saws down the tree . . .
Beginning at the top.

POEM

The wind groans through the trees,
Dragging its heavy cargo
Of coarse fur.

POEM

Small things, soft,
The cotton-tail, the wild dove—
Nesting among thorns.

POEM

Midnight.
This empty page.
                    Wait
For the spider,
The rain.

COMFORT

The night is so long.
Buddha is great!
. . . .
The night is so long. . . .

Buddha is great!
But the night is so
Long, the night is
So
Long.

WEIGHTS & MEASURES

How heavy the weight of the world!
Just now—
On my shoulder—
Enormous
Butterfly.

POEM

The grand days,
No bigger than an hour, maybe,
Rest on my body, sometimes,
Shape of her hand, a
Cloud.

POEM

The stars
The sea
The May Fly
Forever:
Not one day
Older.

POEM

Barnacle-pocked abalone shell—
Warts on a stone.
But within:
Moon-milky nacre . . .
From the toothed margin of the sea—
Who could believe—
The domed lactic interiors . . . .

VISITORS

In the circular voyage of the seashell's song
I hear someone.
Who is calling?
What is it you want me to do?

POEM

In the smallest tidepool
The silence of the anemone
Spells out the secrets
Of the Java Deep.

POEM

To speak is the vice
        of mountains;
To be silent,
        of the sea.

PARABLE

The stick of the blind man
Invents a new darkness.

IN FOG

First: a thickening.
Second: structure of smoke.
Third: rivets anchoring the night.
The bridge
Precipitates
Out of darkness.

INDIAN TERRITORY

The Cottonwood
Sends out its smoke signals.
We are surrounded!

WHAT WE DON'T KNOW KILLS US

Little old deer in the dry crick—
All ganted up.
And beyond him a country mile
Of unfenced corn!

A SEASON

Rain.
Gunfire.
Crows.
        Mist; far; woods.

HALF-LIFE

November darkness . . .
In leaf-ponded woods
The decay of midsummer light.

POEM

Loud November rain . . .
Under the ruins of my autumn garden
Bulbs of the daffodil
Rooted in darkness
In silence.

HOW IT FEELS TO BE SAVED

November empty fields
The icy rains of autumn
The forgotten harrow

THE NEWS AND THE WEATHER

Serene night cold November
Full moon the neighbors
Quarrelling hair greyer almost
Sixty

POEM

All is not well?
All is not well.
All's well then,
Says the world.

POEM

Eclipse
At noonday—
The crow
And the call
Of the crow

POEM

The scarecrow shivering in November corn.
The evening crow crossing over—
United by the first snow.

ANOTHER SEASON

Fall work almost done . . .
Plowing finished and now only
The butchering still to do.

All summer, from the distant house, I heard
A slow grindstone, singing,
Where someone was sharpening the knives.

POEM

Your knife's a most particular guest,
Who lodges colder than a ghost.
Of flesh he's always critical.
Sharpness is not meet in a host.

POEM

Through the fog
The gulls
Carry the sea
Inland

POEM

Lightcrackle
Gullwing
Ice. Print. River.

CROSS COUNTRY FLIGHT

19000 feet.
The shadows of clouds
On clouds.

POEM

I am travelling, travelling . . .
In the direction of the permanent
Contemporary city.

ADVICE

You can neither
Sit on your ass twice
In one
Place or once
In two.

A THEORY

As Thucydides said,
What is history?
Greeks!
Murdering
Greeks

THE EDITOR-POETS' ANTHOLOGY

Quidnunc by Quondam mostly, but
Candidates for eternal fame,
Including one, unforgettable, —
At least to editor What's-His-Name.

TRAVELS OF AN AMERICAN IN SEARCH OF GOD

Sure—
Everyone wants to meet
Him.
But why
In India?

POEM

Revolutionary restructuring needed!
At least of history.
How else can we make the Past
Predictable?

LEGISLATORS OF DARKNESS

Fog over the capitol!
The senators grope homeward.
Larkspur, tree toads
Continue their legislation.

ANOTHER HITCH HIKER SAYS

It's been a long time since I was an American
And Wounded Knee was going on long before it was named
In Alabama or elsewhere
Everybody arrives here
On the Road of Tears, The Road of Wounds, on the Cherokee
Road to the Indian Nation
                                                  prison
                                                        good old Highway
66

POEM

The man treed by the bear:
Everything he owns—
His ass—
Out on a limb.

POEM

The queen of Accident County
Shook a bloody fist at me.
Just about then I realized
The hand she was brandishing at me
Was my own.

*   *   *

O Reality!
O Great Queen!
Where were you when your sister, that bitch Illusion,
Bit off my arm?

ALL'S WELL!

After the storm
Everything in its place my head
Cloudy
         my wet shoes
In the oven

V.

Half-Time at the Funeral

for E. P. Thompson

A NOTE ON *LETTER TO AN IMAGINARY FRIEND*

Someone asks me: "How is *Letter to an Imaginary Friend* like or unlike other long poems?" And someone has written me: "*Letter* is the first post-modernist long poem." Someone else: "You have understood what Whitman meant—that in our time the long poem has got to be biographical."

I don't know what this means. Aren't all poems now "post-modernist"? The great poems of the deep past are third person and "objective." The modernist "long poem" is often not very long, often essentially lyric, and is usually organized around symbols or themes, and the poet is usually at pains to establish "esthetic distance." Of the "long poems" around when I was first at work on *Letter*, Hart Crane's *Bridge* was the one I loved, but it was so far from what I seemed to be doing that I never thought about it. It seemed to me then that there were no models and no theory for the kind of thing that I was doing. That can be frightening and exhilarating.

The writing of long poems has now become a cottage industry. I have seen few of these poems of recent years, but there are enough of them to interest some critic—*something* is going on—even a bibliography would be valuable. Of the "long poems" critics *do* refer to (work of Lowell and Berryman)—these seem to me not single poems at all but collections of related peoms. There is nothing wrong with such collections. What is interesting is that critics seem to *want* and *need* to regard these collections as *long poems*: as if there were some unconscious need for the long poem to *exist*, as if the critics were trying to will it into existence. . . .

How is *Letter* unlike other long poems? In part, perhaps, because it is "pseudo-autobiography." It is *not* simply autobiography. I am very far from believing that all parts of my life are meaningful enough to be usable in the poem. But I believe that all of us live twice: once personally and once as a representative man or woman. I am interested in those moments when my life line crosses through the concentration points of the history of my time. *Then* I live both personally and representatively. I hope to be aware of those moments, because then, I believe, one may be speaking to and for many people.

Some other differences from other long poems (perhaps). *Letter* is not a poem that comes out of the sensibility of the city middle-class intellectual. The city is in the poem, of course, but there is a lot, too, of the backlands and of *place*—that "Dakota" which is central to the poem. There is other material in the poem which seems to me more or less new. Work, for example, is not something which most poets write about. Also communality or solidarity—feelings which perhaps are more important to us than romantic love—never appear in our poetry. Perhaps I have begun to identify them. The attitudes toward these materials, also, are not those of the petty bourgeois intellectual no matter how alienated.

Finally the poem is *political*; it hopes to invent and restructure the past and the future by using the narrative line of the speaker of the poem and events from personal and political-social history to create the "legend" of these times. I am aware of how arrogant this must sound. But I think perhaps this is the only *long* poem to make the attempt.

*   *   *

I am now working on Part Three. Someone asks: "What kind of materials are in One and Two?"

Part One is a narrative which begins with early childhood on a North Dakota farm, goes on to early work experiences, sex, college, and politics in the north and in Louisiana, hitchhiking journeys, the war, and afterwards. It ends in a kind of satori in Los Angeles. Part Two continues the narrative line, picking up themes from Part One and re-seeing them in the light of new circumstances. My note to the book says that Two "is concerned with the offering of evidences for a revolutionary miracle and with elaborating a ceremony out of these materials to bring such a miracle to pass." Part Two begins by repeating the last line of One, and the two parts are a single whole, Book One of the whole poem. Of Part Three, I know very little. I have written some of it and have some longish passages and some bits and pieces which I think belong in projected sections for which I have notes. I think I begin to see the shape it will take. As to the substance—that will be similar to materials in Parts One and Two, but I think the method will be wilder.

There is an inevitable problem with a poem where one's life provides a main narrative track: since the poem shows no sign of stopping, my death (although I have a Two Hundred Year Plan of work) may leave it unfinished. Someone tells me that this is of no consequence, that, after all, "the paintings of Jackson Pollock are completed in the space beyond the picture surface." Cold comfort. I don't like virtues made from necessity. But perhaps others will complete the poem—it seems, in any case, to have a life independent of me in a way that none of my other poems do.

*   *   *

Methods of work? Do I see the structure of the sections of the poem as a kind of collage? It is a useful metaphor, but I see the struture of the sections and of the poem as a whole as being more analogous to the structures of certain films. It is a question of the use of *time*. In any section there will be a general narrative time— the past. But the poem, like some films, makes use of flash-backs and flashes forward, "replays," "subliminal cuts" (phrases from earlier passages or ones which will be developed later on), etc., etc. It would be easy to push this analogy too far, but there are, I think, equivalents of dissolves, fades, etc. So the narrative line is interrupted by other time-lines right up to the immediate present in which the speaker of the poem is sitting in a particular place writing down the immediate words—because the writing of the poem is *also* a part of the subject of the poem. Thus the immediate landscape, what is "outside this window," enters and qualifies or comments on some landscape or circumstance of the past. Similarly the narrative voice is interrupted: occasionally by a remembered quotation, sometimes by the voice of an identified character. Or the tone or persona of the speaker may change: he may have been narrating something from his childhood from a point of view very close to that of the boy in the past; but then the tone may shift radically, and the passage may move into a satirical or fantastic view of the same material, or may bring in elaborations to the scene, or language that is very distant from the point of view of the telling a few lines back. I think this will seldom confuse if the reader will just go on—the poem will soon be back to the initial narrative line. The same way with words or references: they will be made clear by the context, either in their specific meaning or general intent. As the poem goes on, of course, there are occasional references to earlier passages, the repetitions of phrases or lines from earlier parts. It would be best to know those, but generally, again, the context will make them clear. Or so I hope.

Someone asked Godard if he did not think a film should have a beginning, a middle, and an end. Godard is supposed to have answered: "Yes. But not necessarily in that order." The speaker of *Letter* moves around a bit and is interrupted now and then, time shifts, landscapes dissolve into others, but underneath a surface which is fractured and agitated I think the general movement is clear.

The Christmas Section is probably from about the middle of what will be Part III and so has a few things in it which may need to be glossed, though I think they will be clear when the rest of the sections have been completed. In the first place there are all those strange names at the head of the section. These are simply the names, according to medieval occultists, for, first, the powers of the four cardinal directions, then of the "infernal kings of the north," then (Azael, etc.) of the four elements, then of great powers which I associate with the tetragrammaton and the Kachina (of which more later). These powers are ambiguous, and, from a Catholic standpoint, demonic. One of the projects of the poem will be to angelize them. The "Kachina," for the Hopi, is a "God," a deified spirit of great power. According to the Hopi we now live in *Tuwaqachi*, the Fourth World, but we will soon enter *Saquasohuh*, the Fifth World—a much better one. The new world be be signalled by a blue star. Kachinas are also doll figures which are made to symbolize spirit powers. The Blue Star Kachina will help these powers to bring in the new world. All of us should help to make this Kachina. I think of the making of my poem as such an action. In a small way the poem *is* the Kachina.

A few other things. In the Christmas Section #I, the action is simple: a little boy and his father go out to the field in a sled to bring in a load of straw—afternoon the day of Christmas Eve. The narrator tells us this and what it is like to ride behind on a little sled drawn by the big one and what the boy sees at the strawstack and in the fields on the way home. But he is interrupted by various things: the time of year; a vision of the desert landscape of prophecy; a farcical view of the Holy Ghost descending on the Virgin; a surrealistically elaborated fantasy begun by the boy in which his hand leaves him; a meditation in present time when the speaker-writer is looking into his garden; a burlesque of the coming of the Three Wise Men as overlapping film "takes"; some meditation on the importance of using our own hands rather than waiting for salvation.

Christmas Section # II, III and IV were begun and partly written in Lisbon, Portugal, in the revolutionary summer of 1975. There are references to that time in # II of the Christmas Section (and in the parts that follow) and there is a deliberate confusion between Lisbon, Portugal, and the little town of Lisbon, North Dakota.

Any other problems of reference are matters of texture rather than structure, I believe, and should create no real difficulty if the reader will keep the *context* in mind.

from: LETTER TO AN IMAGINARY FRIEND (Part III)

Christmas Section (I)

1.

To go from Cham to Amoymon, Amoymon from Cham from
Sitreal, Palanthon, Thamaar, Falaur, Sitrami—the infernal
Kings of the North . . .
                    Recensions of demons:
                                        Samael, Azazel,
Azael, Mahazael—to look for the fifth element, the Fifth
Season . . .
            Orient, Paymon, Amoymon, Cham
                                        —for the Fifth
Direction
            and six signs of the zodiac still open!
                                        O
Gematria, Notarikon, Temura—Kachina: Yield up the Names!
TET RA GRAM MA TON
                            Coo
Coo.
        "The works of the light eternal are fulfilled by fire". . . .

                        *   *   *

We will proceed southward, pulled by the cold bells
Of the churches, Cham to Amoymon, toward a winter feast of darkness
And light . . .
            Yes.
                    Christmas. Prime. In the savannah of my years,
Nineteen Twenty-one-or-two of the blithe and fooling times
Smooth: buckskin-fit as my little hide to my soul.
Seemed so. Then, anyway.
                        And out to the field at nones,
At the ninth hour of winter song in the falling afternoon light,
Under a sigil of snow and over the december-sintered roof
Of the little river, lifting and lofting our cold voices—
Poor gifts but breath our spirit—calling our holy office
Into the blank white of those fields' now-lost pages
To bring the gold of the summer home for the crèche and crib
And to line the rack of the sled for the trip to Midnight Mass. . . .
That was an easy singing then for the boy's small pagan

97

Heart that followed his then-tall father's magic into
The fields of legitimate joy: all dark soon to be light—
If there was dark at all in the unfailed unaging world . . .
Well, it was a kind and kindly singing I do not deny.
But the world will require a counter-song for those spiritual Entradas:
Enchantments chanted in cantatas to cant open the Third Eye:
(Eye of the World: a wise eye, a worldly wise eye wild
Open for the Fifth Kachina: SAQUASOHUH)
A new jazz, a blues for our old Fourth World
TU WA QA CHI . . .
                        the
                              Hospital . . .

But all this comfort-and-joy began nine months
Earlier—eight months actually, (Virgins Immachinate—unplotting—
Require but eight months' pregnancy. Parthenogenesis anyone?)
Impregnation: April 21, 3:55
P.M. (Hi there, Tomasito!). The Holy Ghost descended
On Mary . . . the long long Fall into the Flesh . . .
There was a traveling salesman no farmer's daughter resists!
—Torose Toro, God's own Taw of the Second Sign,
Holy Square-and-Straight-Shooter to tie and tow her to God,
Great Spook of the Annunciation arriving a month after Gabriel,
H.G., *hydrogen grande*, the sacerdotal hydrogen,
That Always-Was-and-Always-Will-Be of the Steady State system
Of the one and Triune God . . .
                              But hold on! We're a little bit early—
Only two of 'Em so far and eight months to Midnight Mass . . .

Still when the Most High put on his Suit of Blood His mobled
Duds, His mackled and immaculate Zoot, when His Spurs was a-jinglin'—
Then did the Old Gods didder, horripolate, scatter:
—Witches and warlocks skating away on high and windy
Arcs and into the chant sprung nightsky's sudden nave . . .
Learning strange vaportrails, curves unknown to mathematics . . .

These lines will be filled-in in color later by Sputnik,
By the Dog-in-the-Moon (Alvaro wrote that one down),
By the Intercontinental Ballistics Missiles (their loops and crotchets),
By the IFBM (the Interfatality Ballbreaker Missile),
By moonshots and moonshorts, by shooting the sun and bombing the moon:
By putting out all the lights of the bright and morning star . . .

—Sure 'n' ol' Ugly there, jus' as big as his own business!
And there, surely, Old Ugly, the ultimate weapon sits
Gutsgurgling (his special fuel's crofted from blood and sperm)
Big D for Death
    at stool . . .
         sitting on white house lawns . . .
ALL OVA THIS LAND!
      (Orient! Paymon! Amoymon! Cham!) ✝
As in the silos waiting near Grand Forks North Dakota—
O paradise of law and number where all money is armed!
O the Open Eye on the Top of Dollar Mountain: ANNUIT COEPTIS!
IDOLATRY
    IDIOLATRY
      IDEOLATRY

     2.

And still out to pick up that straw in the strum of the afternoon!

I ride in the jingling wake, my small sled tied to the bob,
Jinking along at the back in the field-bound hayrack's furrow
In the deep snow of the river road . . .
         hearing the thrum
Of the cold guitars of the trees and, distant in the dead-still air,
The rumbling of afternoon trains, the shunt and clang of the boxcars
Hunting their sidings in faraway towns at the ends of the wide
World of the winter . . .
     and beyond the jingle of the harness bells,
And the hiss and hush of the runners cutting the deep snow,
As we crossed the river, came the long and compelling call
          magic
Of the whistling distant engines—
      interrupting my father's tune.

Bounding along on my belly on my little drug-along sled,
I knew I was part of the Horizontal, the World of Down.
In the World of Down, everything seemed out of place: as:
Water, now building its winter palace of ice at the well,
(To be lugged to the house in the cold and slopping pails that froze
Our pants into crystal leggins); as flaxstraw, wheatstraw, corn
Always away in some far field when needed at home!
And ourselves too . . .
                    somehow away from the Center . . . in the World
Of Down . . .
               But the World of Up, the Vertical (Christmas reminds us
Once a year!)
                  —*there* we may lift our eyes!
                         (In *that* world
Where no eye looks down; where the earth, perhaps, does not exist
Except for us; where, in their shirts of marble or plaster,
Those bearded wonders and winged wanderers out of a higher
Order, luminous and white, [especially in this so holy
Season]—beings from fields far other and whiter than these
We enter now . . .
              to be entered only by following . . .)

                                 may lift up our
Eyes
     —where Christ on his wooden rocket is braced to ascend!

And here come the Prophets now from the land of Nod!
To follow then: those bearded ones all come from the desert:
A great arc: empty; worn sandstone; silence.
And a louring darkness there where we might have expected light . . .
A few tents, empty, the flaps whipped by the wind.
Abandoned latrines where the sand whispers. A few fires
Where a blackened tin can still simmers a rancid denatured coffee . . .
Is it a railroad jungle here in the Holy Land?
But here is a blacksmith forge where the banked coal still smolders,
And the quenching barrel is ringed with the rainbow flecks of iron
Where the horseshoes hissed and hardened in the kingdom of Tubal Cain . . .
Might as well add in a couple of rolling mills and the odd
Hornacle replicating facility . . . and a jackal or three
Up there in the right-hand corner . . .

100

                                   and a few reeling and indignant
Desert birds or at least their shadows.
                                   Here Number
Is being invented; and its shadow: Law.
                                   Do you feel the cold . . .
And the darkness coming?
                                   And above all else the sense of desertion?
(Those few fellaheen out on the edge have been trained to be silent.)
It will take more than an automobile graveyard to humanize
This landscape. The visions here will all be wrong. Even one
Appletree might change it though . . .
                                   but there is none:
                                                      the wind
                                                           the empty

Dark . . .
          And that landscape persists forever.
                                   Though I am here
In the world of Down: A Helper: bouncing along on my sled . . .

And suddenly there's that ziggurat rising out of the snow!
The strawstack where summer holds: still! in its goldeny heart!
—And my Da beats down the snow and rams a pitchfork in
And the stack-side opens like Adam to the glow of the inner soul
So august-cured and pure.
                         And I will go then and explore
This tent of the tribes of winter all pocked with animal glyphs,
To be hierophant of the fox and the stumbling amanuensis
Of the short stories of fieldmice to whom an Annunciation
Materialized out of the air to fix them numb in their tracks
To be raped and rapt away in ghostly rip-offs by owl-shine,
By hawklight, their poor stuttering last steps a lost
And foxed copy . . .
                    How terrible then to my child's eyes
Were those great mysteries of the air! Signs of the world of Up.

And went then from the strawpile top to the world of Down—
To strawstack tunnels and caves: these were rivers of hunger
Where stray cattle swam through the straw when the nights, full of coyotes,
Barked at the moon.
                        And what were they dreaming then, those Cretan cows,
Eating, their dehorned heads pressed into the side of the summer?
Their chewing mouths . . . black holes open in the universe of blood
Where green things fall forever . . . wells without bottom, graves
Ravening their way forward in the full shine of the stars . . .
—No wonder the coyotes were crying a bottom blues and the moon
Pulled up her skirts—those terrible cows will eat *any*thing!
Will eat up forests, drink rivers so that the bridges fall down!
Will piss on the poorhouse, kick over lanterns and burn down Chicago!
—Leaving behind them a train of round and mysterious stones:
The brown eyes of their frozen dung that glare at the stars
Unblinking . . .
                        and these wintery labyrinths where the bull of summer was

                                                                        eaten.

—All this I read from my strawstack tower where a winter lightning
May yet sour all the bumblebees' honey in a flaring noon
Hung from a dozing and bell-crazed midnight when I, Tom Fool,
Float into the crocodile's mouth of Holy Mother Church
With all my sins on the tap of my tongue and as long as your arm
(An arm that's laced with pin-holes and long snakes like a junkie's)
To be disarmed and tongue-tied there and commanded to climb and to sing
Up a hell-high line of Hail Marys and into the icy rigging
Of the good ship Salvation . . .
                        homeport Jerusalem
                                                outbound
For Beulah Land . . .
                —a little town west
                                —toward the Missouri. . . .

But the lightning does not strike my tower, not yet, and I dance
In the hayrack, building the load, as my laboring darling Da
Lofts up the forkfulls of raw-gold straw like the aureate clouds
Left over from summer.
                  And I, treading my fancy fandango,
My turkey-in-the-straw, while he shouts and laughs and half buries me
Lifting the last of the past year's light—the two of us singing
In a warm winter fable of our summer's work.
                              And done at last
I latch my sled to the right rear bunker and we run for home.

—Sky: changed: now.
                  In the deep catch of the winter:
Dangerous: to turn one's back on Cham, the North and the Northwest
Demon: while the great Siberian highs wheel in and the sly light
Changes without seeming to change and the sky turns blue and bruised
And the icy night of the Blizzard roars down on the wind . . .
Snow showers to the north, and a few clouds, but the weather
Is only closing the grey eye of the evening.

                              Now in the tented
Field the cornshocks tower around me on my tiny sled,
And the cut-back stocks like time tick under my runner's passage.
In that white field, in that grey light, in the world of Down,
Like a land-swimmer, bellyflat on the sled in the flying snow,
I enter a new domain, a new-found-land, like the deme
And doom of a Lapland Dauphin. *Here* is a cold kingdom come—
Place where the local comrades dress wholly in ghostly white.
As instance: the tearaway snowshoe rabbit blowing his cover
With a rapped out curse from a foot the size of a mukluk. (And one
Worn—*sans doute*—by the "red-bearded muzhik from Michigas/Who
Played *folie à Dieu* with the Vichyssoise."
                          How can we stop them?)
And *away* rabbit!
                And now comes the slippery weasel sly and slick
As a fart—in sovereign ermine—priestly—all exclamation—
!Mark! down to the black spot at the end of his tail!
And there go the Prairie Chickens like mad Anarchist Arabic

PRINTERS writing the Koran (or prepared to) across Dakota
And into contiguous Greenland (seduced by the glacier's glabromantic
Belly dances) or writing the Tao in the rows of the dead
Corn.
        A congregation of drunken (ugh!) Noitagergnocs
                                          a prudence
Of confessors
                an excommunication of priests
                                a quarry
Of quarreling tombstones they strut away
                            —talking in Arab.
—And of other birds, aside from the quail and the partridge, there were
Lammergeier, Murres, Snipe (!) Shite Poke and Muscovy Duck
(They don't give a fuck) and Colduck and Thunder Bird
And Guillemot—and musical swans from Nashville who have no names.

And all of them in a most unmerciful and unecumenical goins-on,
Tearing away like sinners snapping at the body of Christ—
(A little empanation here—*and turn on the wine*, the w-i-i-ine)
Mobbilizin' our sacred corn, our sanculotide
Of Fructidore: won from the summer in the Last Days . . .
And, of other birds, there were pheasants which—

_____

_____ *

And the Pheasant leaped out of the tenement of corn like a burglar taken
In flagrante delicto with a cry like an angry bedspring
(Part silver, part bronze, part windchime and part pure galvanized iron:
A gateless gate opening on hinges never been oiled
By a single Koan)—*leaped!* showing his colors, those jewels
Blazing around his neck, in a hellish and helicopterish
Blur and burr of feathers: indignant bandido and banshee!

Coldcocked and donnard by the spunk of that desperate damned desperado
I take comfort from Cousin Owl: now: lifting: silent:
Like a puff of white smoke, so low and so slow drifting . . .
                                    but drifting

_____

*The excised lines were considered (by whom?) as too obscure or Obscene for the eyes of the Gentle Readers.
(Who can they be?)

(Great Snowy Owl) up! and off! and down on the wind . . .
And SUDDENLY doing his Owl magic and DISAPPEARING
INSTANTLY into the absolute white of the vast north winter . . .
—That is (probably) by putting out that one spot of color:
Aii! Eee! merely by closing his eyes . . . .
So thick, the snow, I might put out my hand and lose it!

Seemed

So _____ *

Say what a fortune this hand holds held out at forty below!
Why . . . none . . . Yet.

The hand that went out in the snow

Was lost (it has never come back, never left) and for forty years
Has wandered the desert.

Yes siree! It's a *fact*.

And in them same environs

Where, a while back, you may have noticed them tents and them jackals—
Sand drifting . . . open latrines—

a forge still hot . . .

Deserted.

Oh, yes, He has been there too, this Hand,

A-loose in the landscape of Prophecy always here or hellswhere,
(Though it seemed to me that He might forget how to find His way
Home; or that He might, like a thief, steal into my pocket
And forget to let me know He was back—and I'd be afraid
To feel for Him there, that much-traveled Hand, that voyager, hidden
In my worn jacket—or He might stay away for years and turn up
In my Christmas stocking, playing with all my toys and breaking them,
Groping the apples, assaulting the oranges, returned so wise,
Or cynical—I wouldn't know what to do with a Hand like that!)
But: I put out my hand . . .

—lost at once in the blinding snow . . .

---

*This line was omitted by publisher for failure to fulfill the norms of that School of Poetry best known by the ideogram ⊙. This ideogram (known in Academic and Antiacademic circles and squares as the Poet's Sign) is generally translated: no-hearum, no-seeum, no-sayum. Nevertheless (see above):

And so the forty—more or less—years of the wandering
Staking a claim now and again but continually dowsing
For secret water—for it seemed that everyone was dying of thirst
In those ancient contemporary landscapes where the Hand was hired and fired
Often: as a foreign-born Agitator and oft-foiled Révolutionnaire.
But persisted, this Hand; blazing the trees toward the Secret Country,
Setting the type of the Manifesto, and picking up the fallen gun.
Yes, this Hand has wiped away other tears than those of its owner . . .
This is the hand they kicked out of all the Academies and Antiacademies,
(Still building them fires and steering the dowsing wand).
Been fired by cattlemen and sheepmen and gone to live with the outlaws:
(Hole-in-the-Wall his address; letterdrop on the owlhoot trail).
And was agent (Haganah; '47) before they set up that
Arab shooting gallery on the Great Plains of Texaco
In the Gaza Strip: this Hand has shook down several Safe Houses
(Though not enough) and has levitated high as Mohammed's Coffin
(Suspended between Earth and the Eschatological) to ask forgiveness
In his own poor language—that of the Tuatha de Danaan—
Which (alas!) the Prophet did not speak. (And this is
The Hand's general experience with prophets—hello, Allen
G.!)
        But persisted, this Hand, and put out numerous fires
(Some he had started) and put His Self in the eternal blaze
Often: to carry coals to Old Castle.
                                 This Hand has
Increased temperatures in reptiles and some reptilian critics (Hi
Poor Richard!) and increased the Kelvinical and Thermidorian reactions
(Can't win 'em all!) of country and city cunt, and has stroked
(Surreptitiously) the Venus de (blank) and one ass even more classic.

| Classical Ass |
| Is Hard to Pass |

This is the Hand that dreamed it was a foot and walked around the world on
                                                                water!
That went to Oxford and found a bull; that went to the Louvre
To learn how to feel: that has snapped off the heads of marauding pheasants!
This is the Hand that is still searching for Itself in my pocket!
This is the Hand that glommed from the wind a four thousand dollar bill from
                                                     Palmer Thompson!

(Senescent Capital accumulation—see Karl Marx).
This is the Hand that wrote on the blazing walls of Greece the blaze Z!
That was twice cut off at the wrist for begging alms in Almsbury!
This hand was buried at Wounded Knee in a fit of skeletal abstraction!
This is the Hand that carried the rifle (age 10) to assassinate the local banker!
This is the Hand that lit the chandeliers of all the underground seas!
This Hand is the author of McGrath's Law: *All battles are lost but the last!*

This is the Hand that removed the liounes from the menaces to Daniel!
This is the Hand that wrote the words
                         that warned the King
                                    who prepared the menaces to Daniel!
This is the Hand that built the wall
                    where the words appeared
                                 that frightened the King
                                    who prepared the menaces to Daniel!
This is the Hand that ripped down the wall
                    where it wrote the words
                              that destroyed the king
                                    who prepared the menaces to Daniel!
MENE MENE TEKEL UPHARSIN!
                    This is the Hand

Now why was such a *gentle* Hand so hunted?
                                   He wants
Only to hold the apples that grow outside this window . . .

Why?

Because of the Three Lustful Vegetables who hated Him!
Because of the lack of disorder in early surrealists' surly lists and last lost orders!
Because he was born so far from home!
And also because his best girl never learned how to write!
Because of the disappearance of the Third International!
Because (so they say) of the electronic pollution of birdsong!
And because (finally) (so they say) hell is overpopulated!
And has moved (furthermore: so they say) to Chicago!
And finally because that summer cows' tongues turned to wood
And we had to shoot them between their large moist eyes
With tiny rimfire cartridges made by a subsidy of DuPont.
And finally because the banker George P. never came by   107

Where I lay in ambush, with my brother Jimmy and our .22 rifles.
And finally
          and finally . . .
                    and finally.
                              etc.
                                   etc.
                                        etc.
Because from forms of freedom the spiritual relations turn into
Fetters of the spiritual forces. Then comes the epoch
Of theomorphic revolution.
                              But still this Hand *did* come back . . .

A salt script, *lettre de cachet* . . .
                              "and *he* is to *read*—
   Here!—in these *sweatswamps* of his *Hand*—in these *llanos* and *pampas*,
   In the quicksands of his palm, in that graph whose line is continually falling
   (Graph, we may add, where neither abscissas nor ordinates can apply)
   —In this *thing* without geometric form to its shape or its name
   (Vectorless and parameterless as a eunuch)—without a fri'nd in the world!
   You expect this *boy* here to read his fate in his Hand
   (Which furthermore may be fondling the apples in his Christmas stocking!)
   To read—*here*—in them Sand Hills and them Bad Lands!—
   His *fate*? To read there in the alkali flats in the palm
   Of his hand, in that earthquake country—I ask: you expect him to *read* . . .?"

Yes.
     I say it is all in our hands.
                    It is in all
Our hands' hard-lines-and-times and cold fatalities.

And all in our Christmas stocking: the one we seldom look into . . .
And meanwhile what of our Hand?
                    Oh, He is home,
                              been home—
At six fifteen south eleventh across the Red River from Fargo!
This hand is searching this white page of that distant snow—
Like a blind hawk hunting the trackless emptiness ahead—
Searching for your hand to hold while we write this down together—

3.

Apples.
        Outside this window, from the top floor of this house,
At this desk, at five twenty-three on a fine June morning,
In that light, in this waking, I find in these
Abandoned latitudes and fake doors into the slatternly
Weather (blowsy and whorish that will hold us another year
In the Fasching and false gestures of festival thermometers) I find these
Apples.
        Up in a tree.
                Down from my desk
                        —where else?
Nothing special about them.
                    They are of two kinds:
One which can make pies—with the proper human ingredients;
The other an ornamental crab
                    —and I see one bloom
Still! Left over from Spring six weeks ago, to what
End?
        Spray "like a rapid branch of music"—*those*
Flowers . . .
          so late . . .
                   those most tendentious and irregular flowers!

I think I have heard them before. But I won't ask *when,* as I look
Past them over the frozen coulee where we haul in the straw—
(You remember we went out for straw and lost a singular hand?
The good right hand was it? Or the sinister left of darkness?
The lost hand of feeling—the left and dreaming hand?).

_____

*It may be that these lines (and there may be many more than suggested here) constitute the key to the whole
poem—and perhaps to *all* poems, or at least to those where unseen collaborators of present and future have
added lines of their own.

—So: apples. I "love" them, rounding, and that belated bloom,
Even if *love* is in quotes.
                              (It is hard to know *how*
Love *is* these days, or what should be its proper object . . .
—What is there, Comrades, (I ask) but love and the class struggle?)
Hubble-bubble-bubble (saith the "poet of love") in his latest book.
But I feel tender toward them anyway, those last late blooms,
And special solidarity now toward the proletarian Apple
Lifting—*how* does it do it?—seems . . . easy—like a fountain—
That great freight and weight of the late and ripening fruit . . .
Lifting toward heaven in the virgin morning—borne up by birdsong!—
Apples for my Christmas stocking fifty—only fifty!—years early or late!

                    *   *   *

We bring in the straw in an evening clear and pearly.
                                              Open
To all the light of the wide, wild, woolly west . . .
Into which I am looking now . . .
                              at those patient apples . . . and into
My garden:
"Larkspur, lupine, lavender, lantana, linaria, lovage" . . .
—Sounds like a season in L's: too far from anywhere ever
To get home at all . . .
                    But here we have got to the P's
                                        Peonies
Anyway. To Patience plant and Im-
                              patience
                                   and Jack-in-the-Pulpit—
Plants that will grow in the dark (or at least in the shade) and Paradisaical
Apples! It seems better.
                    As we go on from the P's to the Q's—
(In the shade: where I am: growing eucharistical bread)
And Quince: apple of the first Garden
                                   —I grow it here . . .
Here!
     On this desk!
                    World-apple and apple of my eye . . .
Eve's apple, the Quince was—world with a bite taken out:
For which I offer this weight of paper as receipt and roadmap
Forward toward the only Eden it is possible to find and farm.

110

I turn over my paperweight now as a puff of hot wind blows
These winter pages. And inside that glass apple or tear,
A fall of woolly snow is clouding the gold of my trees . . .

But west from this little garden, over the coulee, the light
Hardens toward Christmas Eve.
                              In that gone time
                                                in this
Light we wait for supper and the Three Wise Men . . .

> The Coming of the 3 Weiss Men
> A Tale for Good Little (Red) Indians
> And other (Colored) Minorities . . .

Gentle Reader: Once upon a Time, in the Anywhere that is Dakota . . .
You can imagine about what it would have been like out there:
Lift the window on Canada and let in a little snow—
Some cyclonic widdershins here, if you please!—and some of that cold
That sent Sam Magee to the furnace with Shadrach, Meshach and Abednigo,
And a bit of smell from the lignite that burns in the pot-belly stove . . .
And the woman, working, of course—milking the cow, maybe,
Or making butter (best to have her inside here) or cooking
(What?) Praties, maybe. Or if they're Norwegian—lefse.
Not a bad angle there. *Cut.* Through the window we see her

(*That dreaming farmwoman's face*—SHE IS IRONING CLOTHES: I KNEW IT!)

Thinking of sunny Trondheim and the troll that took her virginity
(*Make a note back there somewhere that she's pregnant and near her time*)
While Sven is reading his newspaper: *The Scandinavian Panther*
And we see in LONG SHOT: HER POINT OF VIEW: away down the
                                                                coulee

These . . . well . . . *kings*, sort of, mopin' 'n' moseyin' along
Towards . . .
            "Ole?"
                        (*I* know it's Sven but *she* has forgotten!)
"Ole"
        "Yah?"
                "Some strangers comin' up the coulee . . ."
                                                "Yah"

"Look like three *kings* . . ."
                    "Yah"
                                   "Or could be, maybe, the Prairie Mule
'N' a coupla lonesome deadbeats staggerin' home from the Sand Hills . . ."
"Y-a-a-ah."
                    "For Jasus sake, man dear, if not for me own,
Put down that poteen! Here come the holy season fallin' upon us
Like an avalanche of hard Hail Mary's and yerself down on all fours
Drunker than Paddy's pig—"
                                   "But I'm tellin' you woman I see 'em—"
"And meself with a belly as big as a barn and me time come—"
"Mary! it's three *kings* I see!—Unless it's Fergus
Of the golden cars . . . and Coohooligan . . . and wan of thim other ten million
Famous kings us Irish is famous for. Or else . . . maybe . . ."
"Or else?"
                    "Or else Bill Dee and the Prairie Mule and maybe . . ."
"Maybe?"
                    "Some other lonesome deadbeat staggerin' home from the Hills . . ."
"Y-a-a-ah?"
                    "I tell ya I see it right here in the Book of the Blue Snow,
Woman! And them comin' on like Buster's Gang! 'N' it *is*
Bill Dee! wid a Japanese portable television!—on which I see—"
"Television ain't been invented yet, Ole."
                                   Well Jasus woman it's _____"
Cut *Cut* CUT!
            But it *is* Bill Dee—
With a portable T.V.
                    On which you may see Bill Dee, coming
Up the coulee with a portable T.V. on which you may see
Bill Dee with a portable T.V. coming . . .
                                   Get the idea?

We may deduce from this that the Wisemen heve *not* come—or
We may deduce that the *true* Wisemen have not come *or*
We may deduce that the true Wise Men have not
Come—for the poor.
            Yet.
                    Or have come and have been forgotten . . . .

Let's interview Bill Dee . . .

                 "Hi, Bill! I see
You're still viewing the world through that obfuscatory glass eye—
Whatta ya see out there? Why are ya here? Tell me!"
"Why *not*? Put a glass eye in yer head—and many have 'em—I tell ya,
'n' ya'll wander the wide world long, wild wonders to see!
I'm just walkin' along 'n' I come across these two mopers
Wanderin'! A water-witcher 'n' a witch-watcher 'n' neither of 'em
Could find water or witch in a ten gallon hat and *it* fulla stud piss!"

(I hear the heavy trains of the sea coming in to the anywhere
Stations of sand and salt . . .
                —but: back to the subject!)
"'n' so, after a cold crossin' we come to their guards."
—"Guards?"
         "You don't think everythin's pertected?—and this a hierophany!
—Anyway: Guard says: 'Advance. And gimme the counter sign!'
'n' *I* says *Countersign*? What the fuck you talkin' about
Buster? 'n' he says: 'Right on! *Advance one countersigner!*'
'n' here I am! 'n' whatta ya think of *them* apples?"
Well.
     It could have been someone like Bill Dee . . .

                         we were so
Lost . . .
     Did Christ die . . .
               waiting for the three Wise
Men?
     Or is he still waiting,
             shivering in some
                   lost
Sheepfold?
       Corral?
          Or the hencoops which we have prepared for his final
Coming?

     Under us a lattice, thin as a molecule, grows
Instantaneous—formed (just under our feet as we flash
Forward over our world) like the forming of winter ice
Over the river . . .
         and we skate onward carolling:

"Over the winter ice!"
                    Never aware how thin
That winter ice is . . . formed for an instant under our feet
Then vanishing . . .
                    Or in summer as waterwalkers we skate
The dogday rivers . . .
                    the thin skin of the water holding
An instant that is ours forever as we rush out to the stars.

But it's thin ice, or thin water, anywhere you look . . .
I turn over this weight of paper, this paper weight and the world
Dissolves in snow . . .
                    over my garden . . .
                                        what do you think
Of *them apples*?
                    If I blink a tear away the world will
Disappear!
                    But I will not.
                                        Nostalgia is decayed dynamite.
                                                        Cham.
Amaymon. Orient. Paymon.
                                        In all the rose of the compass
No charge is left.
                    Now we must lift up our hands . . .
                                                        to ourselves . . .
Already it's nearly too dark to say anything clearly.

CHRISTMAS SECTION (II)

1.

. . . too dark to say anything clearly, but not too dark
To see . . .
        one foot in early twilight, the other in snow,
(Now failing away in the western sky where a fair star
Is travelling our half-filled trail from the still, far, field—
O rare light!—trailing us home toward the farmhouse lamp)
We go:
      home:
          and then, with a shout!, my brother Jimmy
Leaps! And cleaves to my back on the little sled:
                    and we're home . . .

             *   *   *

But not too dark to see . . .
            It is snowing in Lisbon,
                Tomasito!
(At the corner of *Rua do Karma* and Rolling Stone Square,
Where I'm living and loning and longing for you.)
                  Portuguese winter!
A snow of leaflets falls from the hot and dumbstruck sky.
Midnight Mass for the Fourth and Fourteenth of July, Tomasito!
Or maybe the snow of Pentecost: the leaflets speak in *all* tongues
Of men and angels—and maybe it's time to change
               angels . . .
Still . . . *not* too dark to see . . .
           (—was right *here*
Somewheres—place we got lost . . .)
            And I *do* see:
               here:
                 clearly
(Having third sight) *primero* (and aside from all the political
Palindromes) I see the beautiful girls of the Poor,
(More beautiful than all the nineteen thousand Marys) rusting
Under the hailing and merry slogans of the Tetragrammaton
Of the Revolution
         —each Throne, Counter-throne, Power and Dominion
Of the hierarchy of those fallen angels signed with Hammer & Sickle!

They rust and rest—or their simulacra or holy pictures—
Where I saw them once before, among the foreign money,
On the back walls of earlier bars and wars . . .

                                        their asses
Widen . . .

            icons . . .

                    calendar queens . . .

                            (And Cal's girl, too . . .)
Some have wakened to fight in the man-killing streets, but these, enchanted,
Dream-chained in the burning palace of Capital, slumber . . .
They sleep where Custer sleeps and only Keogh's horse
Is alive . . .

            over cheap bars where pão and vinho verde
Have not changed into their bodies of bread and wine . . .

                                                Not
Changed, yet, but changing: for also in those darkbright streets
I can hear the guns (seven, twenty-seven, seventy-five)
Of the July Days . . .

                (though they haven't started shooting yet).

                                        And the bells
On the trucks of soldiers and armed workers.

                                But few of the latter—
Alas . . .

        Like the girls, the Workers' Councils (soviets) are resting
Or rusting . . .

            —Though they and the damned poor are wrestling for the
                                            Body of Good
Through the ten thousand parties of the Revolution:
                                    there
                                        in the shouting
Streets that all end in the cold sea.
                            No time!
For love!
        (Though this is a kind of love.)
                                It is time! (they sing!)
                                            Time!

116

(And the bells clang from the rushing trucks and the tall towers)
Time!—to change angles and angels and to reinstate
Cham, Amoymon, Marx, Engels, Lenin, Azael,
Stalin, Mahazael, Mao, Sitrael—Che-Kachina—
O yield up the names of the final Tetragrammaton!—
Time! to make sacred what was profane! Time! Time!
Time!
         to angelize the demons and the damned . . .

2.

And we, of the damned poor, trot our frost-furred horses
Into the barn where beyond the glinting lantern, a blessed
And a steamy animal sleep is clotting into a night
Dreamless, perhaps, or, if blurred by dreams, it is green as summer
And the hay that burns there—a cattle-barn night, star lighted
By rays from the deadwhite nailheads shining in their rime-laced albs.

The yard is corralling the darkness now, but Orient offers
A ghost-pale waning moon host-thin in the wan and failing
Light:
The sun that brief December day now gone
Toward topaz distances . . . of mineral afternoons
Beyond the Bad Lands . . .
                              toward Montana . . .
                                        the shandy westernesses . . .

And we three (who are now but one in the changed and changing
Dark of my personal fading and falling world) we three
Hand in hand and hand in heart sail to the house—
My father has lent me the light so we can go hand in hand,
Himself between us, the lantern brighter than any moon!

Indoors, my mother bends over the stove, her face rosy
In the crackling woodfire that winks and spits from an open lid.
And we are *all* there, then, as we were, once,
On the planet of sadness in a happy time. (We did not, then,
Miss you, Tomasito, an unsuffered age away
Waiting for all my errors to make me one time right.)

117

And so I will name them here for the last time, who were once
Upon the earth in a time greener than this:
My next brother Jim, then Joe, then my only sister, Kathleen,
Then Martin, then Jack, the baby.
                                        Now Jim and Jack have gone
Into the dark with my mother and father. But then—
                                                            Oh, then!
How bright their faces shown that lamplit Christmas Eve!
And our mother, her whole being a lamp in all times and weather . . .
And our father, the dear flesh-gantry that lifted us all from the dark . . .

        [In that transfiguring light, from the kitchen wall, a Christ
        Opens his chest like an album to show us his pierced heart
        As he peers from a church calendar almost empty of days.
        Now: say, then, who among you might not open your flesh
        On an album of loss and pain—icons of those you have loved
        Gone on without you: forever farther than Montana or sundown?
        No Christ ever suffered pain longer or stronger than this . . .]

So let me keep them now—and forever—fixed in that lost
Light
        as I take the lantern and go down the stairs to the cellar
In search of the Christmas apples cold in their brimming bin.
There, as deep in the hull of a ship, the silence collects
Till I hear through the dead-calm new-come night the far bells:
Sheldon . . .
            Enderlin . . .
                        bells of the little towns
                                        calling . . .
Lisbon . . . North Dakota . . .

                        [Yes, I hear them now
        In this other time I am walking, this other Lisbon, Portugal—
        Bells of the Revolution, loud as my heart I hear
        Above the continuous bad-rap of the urine-colored sea.
        Beside which I am walking through that snow of July leaflets
        In search of the elusive onion to make the home-done sandwich
        Herbaical and vegetable and no doubt even healthy, and certainly
        Hearty-seeming (in mind's tongue) after fifteen K's and quais
        A la recherche de cebolla perdue:

Vegicum Apostolicum
Herbibable sancti et ecumenicabable . . .
Meanwhile
I die on the vine waiting for news from you, Tomasito,
Waiting for the angel, waiting for news from heaven, a new
Heaven, of course—and a better world in birth! *here*:
Under the changing leaflets under the flailing bells.]

And the bells of Sheldon carry me up the steep of the stairs,
My feet set in a dance to be bearer of these cold apples,
The fairest fruit of our summer labor and harvest luck.
I lay them out on the lamplit table. On the gleaming cloth,
In the dreamy gaze of the children they glaze in a lake of gold!

O high wake I have said I would hold!
It has come all unknown:
Unknown!
And my blood freezes
to see them so:
In *that* light
in this
light
each face all-hallowed
In the haloing golden aura shining around each head!

And how black and stark these shadows lean out of the hollow dark
To halloo and hold and hail them and nail them into the night
Empty
—its leaden reaches and its cold passage
empty . . .

And so, at that last supper, in the gold and blood of their being,
So let me leave them now and forever fixed in that light.

To go from Cham to Amoyman!
                                Toward Midnight Mass!
                                                And the frost
Filing the iron of the runners or the runners filing the snow!
It sets our teeth on edge, that gritting and steely protest
Against our going. But we go all in joy! In joy
Our holy carols and catcalls collect from the coulee hills
Their coiling and icy answers like echoes drawn from the stars!

Initiatory ceremonies toward a feast of illusionary light!
The holy words rise cold in the ghost-shapes of our breath,
Our little smokes and fires that lift the words-made-flesh
Into the eye of heaven, the bone glare of the moon
Her celestial pallor
                        deathshine . . .
                                        (All that the priests have left
Of the warm and radiant Goddess who once held all our hands!)
And rise as well to the dark demons stirring around us
Pale in their faint fire whose dream on this night of nights
Is again to be born and burn with that flame the world once was
Before the abstract light of the Father's Heavenly Power
Put out the eyes of the stars and drained the life from the moon.

Cold Heaven, now! The alienating Pale
Of the Priestly Power Trust, God's Own Monoply Light,
Has fenced off our fallen world, all . . .
                                        —from our true sight—
Insight: all dark now and the motherly magic
That once had opened our eyes and hearts to Brother Flower
And Sister Star and Brother Bear and Deer and all
Sisters and brothers—
                        Samael
                                Azazel
                                        Azael
                                                Mahazael
Brothers and sisters: fire, water, earth, air . . .
Dark . . .
                But the Father offers the Son, that bearded foxfire,
And those ten-watt dusty street-lamps, the Saints, in place of the inner eye!
Oh! Orient, Paymon, Amoyman, Cham! Help me reject them!

Palanthon, Sitrael, Thomarr, Sitrami! Send a true Prophet!

"... and I will mercy themfella b'long Her
                                        no chop
    Beef b'long all them poor fella bastards
                                    no chop
    Poor himfella ox nor himfella wife her child
                                        no chop
    Themfella soul b'long 'em nor themfella labor
                                            I will

Mercy themfella b'long mercy
                                            I will

Virtue themfella b'long virtue
                                    I AM NOT

COME TO CALL THE RIGHTEOUS!"

And other things of the sort . . .
                            "an ancient compelling music"
                                                            I
Hear it:
        around me now:
                        our songs for the wrong ear:
Rising
        up: hymnfella b'long himfella Jehovah . . .
An ancient music and never false, the rounddance
Of the living and the dead and the flowering and laboring world we sing:
Carolling loud our solidarity,
Offering lauds to the wrong god journeying joyfully
Toward
        Deathlehem
                in the ma'a'rannin'!
                                    Singing!
Oh, sing—
        From the flat prairie issues the Pragmatist,
        And from the mountain top the crazy seer;
        But who will marry, across the iron year,
        That raving Virgin who will not be kissed?

121

                                        Oh, sing . . .
"Of no school of prophets, yet am I a prophet's son!"
O sing

                            *   *   *

And all of us off for Sheldon at seven below to save
Our sinburned souls—carolling bravely along!
                                        And the sledteam
Jingling the harness bells! Oh, singing services! Under
The blaze of the wandering Houses of stars, those fiery tribes
In their nightlong trek to nowhere their wasting and constant light
Shifting . . .
                    They reel and plunge away, and the constellations
Sway and change their shapes as the bobsled cants and pitches,
Rolling like a small ship through the drifts on the coulee hills.
Those dancing stars are all we can see from where we sit,
As if in a well, in the sled-box bottom, the wooden sides
Rise four feet high around us like blinds, cutting our view
Of all but heaven . . .
                    and my father,
                                who, on the high seat,
Speaks to the horses in the calming croon they know and respect,
While the cold of the winter solstice weathers his loving face.

The rest of us, our eyes to the reeling and drunken stars
Upraised, burrow into the straw on the sledbox bottom,
Cocooned in wool and fur: in sheepskin, doeskin;
In horse blankets and horse-*hide* blankets; in buffalo-robes
And buffalo-coats; in pigskin, mink, raccoon and weasel—
In our animal palliaments all togged out; in academicals and regimentals
Happily habilimented: in paletot, dolman, sagum and chlamys;
In yashmak, in haik and huke, in tabard, redingote and wraprascal
Accoutered:
                    —fillibeg plain or swathed in ermine smalls!

Shadowed by a cloud of animal souls we progress slowly
South.
            Moon dogs and a ring around the moon . . .
I see them there like sundogs left over from afternoon
When we went for straw.
                            In the sledbox bottom charcoal smoulders—
            ("The works of the Light Eternal shall be fulfilled by fire!"
            O the slow burning of time in the cells, Tomasito!)
—Smoulders in the little footwarmer—an incense across the night.
Tintinnabulation of harness bells . . .
                                    and the silver
Thurible of the moon . . .
                            and the moon dogs' holy offices . . .

                    *   *   *

(*Days with the sunfall valorous and the nights rusty with sleep*
In the smell of the small rain . . .)
                                I have been dreaming of summer
When the sled, stopping, wakes me.
                                I hear a strange voice . . . dream
Again:
        (*of milky lightning, miniature and faint,*
Of summers still . . .
                    and lorn . . .
                            by musky woods . . .
                                        ensorcelled . . .)

And wakening sharply I wonder what time of year I am at
And where I am.
                    Voices faint and far arrive
Where I burrow in animal sleep.
                        I recognize my father
And the voice of another man that I ought to know but I don't.
Then: Midnight Mass, I remember; the sled; the kids; my mother.
Tree shadows pass. I try to guess how far we've gone,
How long I slept . . . ('cause I'm a fast dreamer, a dream
Champ: and I dream to the left or the right, of future or past
Equally—I'm Rip Van Winkle of a century still to wake up) . . .

So—full awake I rise from the fur of my sleep to the cold,
And go to the front of the sled to stand at my father's back.
On the seat beside him is the man we stopped to pick up
When my dream broke in half. But this is a summer man:
(If only in name) Looie La Fleur—in full verbal
Bloom—muttering to himself or the night at large: talking
To himself or the weather—he is not always sure which is which.
The chime and rhyme of the horseshoes ring on a roof of ice—
We have come to the dark of the river trees, no farther.

                                                    The moon
Etches their coarse lightning of shadow across the snow,
Where a wooden cannon of cold explodes in the heart of an oak
Its wintry thunder.
                    The river is frozen brink to bed
Almost, and the fish will be rising and rafting up where the springs
Open an icy window and the deer come down to drink
Through the fox-lighted brush where the coyote sings . . .
                                                    faithful . . .
—How faithful these confederates hold to their single lives!

And faithful the little river (where we go forward over
The winter ice) rings us its carol; as, far and faithful,
It steers toward the starfish-lighted, the alewife-breeding sea . . .
In the dur season.
                    And we, faithful or foolhappy in folly,
Follow
        skating on thin ice or thin lives—
Honorable travelling in hard times—
                                    rebelling . . .
                                            enduring . . .
                                                    O!
Long, long have we dured and dure we longer shall!

                    *   *   *

Carolling, over the winter ice we go . . .
                                ("*I'll take you*
Over the river" . . .
                I said, once).
                            (*And* I say . . .
                                        Now

Only . . . slip your foot free of the stone
                                my darlings
                                        my dear ones . . .)

We have come to the Ambush Place where I shall make that promise
In five or six years sled time in my future that's past
Now . . .
                "But there's always another one comin' while the trains still run!"
(My father's Anarcho-Communist-Wobbly wisdom tells me.)

The Ambush Place . . .
                        when my journeying soul is five years older
Than the Christmas boy I was—or six years maybe—(it's only
The legend that counts) a long way from Midnight Mass . . .
                                                In the Ambush Place
We lay
        my brother Jim and I
                                in my summer confusions
Where the bridge crosses the Maple River south of the coulee—
We lay
        with our .22's and our terror
                                Agrarian Reformers
Waiting for our local kulak-cum-banker to cross the bridge.
He was throwing us off his land and we intended to put him
Six feet under: with some point twenty-two
Hundreths holes to ventilate the closed system of His Corporate
Structure
        (O Falaur, Sitrami, Sitrael, Thamaar—aid!)

Anarcho-juvenile expropriation of the expropriators!
O infantile disorder!
                But generous too, I think:
                                the innocent
Hope: "the open and true desire to create the Good."
He never came—(we have waited a long time for the Kulak
To come into our sights!).
                        We lay
                                trembling
                                        afraid of our fear . . .

And wait there still I suppose in some alternate world, wondering
If we will shoot
                    in the possible future
                                        wait
                                        wait—
("We know everything about the universe except what is going to happen
Next," saith the poet. [Charlie Potts]).

                                                        He did not come
That day . . .
                    (And we must always start *Now!*
                                        Now!
Here: where the past is exhausted, the future too weak to begin.)

We lay there
                    powerful
                                        I remember the summery smell
Of the river
                    birdcall
                    O powerful
                                        I remember
                                                        smelling
The yellowy, elecampane raggedy-headed flowers . . .

                                        *   *   *

"Don't go barefoot to a snake stompin'!
                                        There's no friends
In Wolf City!"
                    So . . . we go on—passage by night,
By water—but the river is frozen and nothing is charmed or changed
By our little crossing . . .
                                        (as, in faery stories: crossing
A stream changes all)
                                        as little was changed in that other Crossing
Where we went over the Potomac in the "siege of the Pentagon":
In '68 I think it was: and got into Second
Bull Run by some kind of historical oversight . . .

126

A confusion of waters:
                    the Maple . . .
                              the Potomac . . .
                                        —and the Susquahanna!
In the Cooperstown hospital, I walked the ward, wondering
If I would continue.
                    Midnights, looking out where that river,
No more than a ditch but deep and black in the moonlit snow,
Flowed out of the Glimmerglass . . .
                              (Cooper's river.)
                                        And flowed back
Into romance: the deep, heroic and dishonest past
Of the national myth of the frontier spirit and the free West—
Oh, nightmare, nightmare, dream and despair and dream!

A confusion of waters, surely, and pollution at the head of the river!
Our history begins with the first wound: with Indian blood
Coloring the water of the original springs—earlier, even:
Europe: the indentured . . .
                    And the local colorist *still* going back:
To the Past: to HEADwaters and HEARTlands (he thinks):
To camp out in the American Dream (beside still waters!):
To atomic cookouts: "Bring your own nigger or *be* one!" (remember?)
To the false Past . . .
                    Which we must restructure if we're to create
The commune
          and the round dance . . .
                              Kachina . . .
                                        the Fifth Season . . .

The National Past has its houses, but their fires have long gone out!

4.

We have crossed the waters . . .
                    And I go back to rebuild my dream . . .
    [Once more in the river hills the cons of summer come!
    The navy of False Grape swims out of the greening trees
    And the cold fox of the winter has changed the brass of his brush!
    The hard edge of the water that lately broke in my hand
    Vanishes: ice gone out and the shallows stippled with fish.
    The roads of fur and fetlock where the hungry deer wandered
    Close. Close. And the supernal green rolls in!]

I wake from the old dream of Eden I know so well . . .
All nature ample and benign:
                  watersong
                         birdsong
                                 the paradisal
Green:
        in which all seasons and all class colors drown.
Then, mornings, rising, hungry, from the milk of sleep,
I searched my angry beast throughout the world's five fields.
But it is the fifth I'm concerned with: and the Fifth Season, the Fifth
World . . .
        SAQUASOHUH
                    —*now*, as I make this Kachina
In a bad season: *here*
              when winter has come into my travelling eye
And wrinkled autumn has entered the dry skin of my hands . . .

But I can remember my anger as I searched the green and golden
Promise of the world I tried to regain at the Ambush Place
And anger sustains me—it is better than hope—
                            it is *not* better than
Love . . .
        but it *will* keep warm in the cold of the wrong world.

And it was the wrong world we rode through then
                       and ride through *now*—

Through the white field of this page
                              (where the bells of Lisbon . . .
                                                      Portugal . . .
North Dakota . . .
                    ring all our times the same in the need for change).

And, on the white page of this field, a thin snow,
Falling, does not change the moonlight or damp the sound
Of the screeling stridulation of the sled-runners, their iron screed.
We have climbed the round of the river hills
                                        where fear collects
Like starlit dynamite in the heart-stopping track of the wolf,
Past the labyrinth of malefic ions in the sleep-struck den of the snake—
Past animal wisdom—
                        and now through the open pasture gates
(The open gates of the winter!) we race at a ringing trot!

And so we go over that dead time on the iron-white fields
And past the spring where the last of the deer come in, and past
The little graveyard where even the cemetery stones are going
Underground.
            [Place where in time my baby brother—now
        Sleeping in our mother's arms—will hunt; and the great cock-
        Pheasant will rise in his feathery mystery, his shimmering mail
        Dew-diamonded and with his neck bright-beaded, and I . . .
        Thunder-hearted, unable to fire . . .
                                but my brother, Jack,
        Grown then, and himself only a few years behind
        His own death—
                        Deadeye Jack downs him with a .22!]
And so past the Old Kennedy Farm where we will live
(Later) and past Lasky's (the "Polish-Bohunk") and past
The place of that "morphodike" who, when he is rich, will found
The first tractor graveyard in these "wild lands of the West"
To quote Bill Dee.
                (And why not? It's Christmas!

And there are moon dogs like the sundogs of afternoon—
Remember? Before all these loves and deaths, when we went for straw
On this page of a field or a field of pages and found these odd
Birds?
        The ones which may be rising now, over
This sled, this cargo of singing dead and dying
                        the birds
        Of that afternoon six hours or six thousand years ago?)
And so to Sheldon where the bells of Christmas are slowly drifting
Their iron clouds of sound and song across the night . . .

                  *   *   *

It is in winter we see the world as it is: wild:
Inhuman . . .
        then the buildings (that once in summers past
Nosed like slow ships into the calico winds,
Their sails full of cicadas, voices the color of gold)
Then, in that bone-breaking cold, the houses that seemed deep-rooted
Snap off at the knees, at the first joint, as the darkening
World freezes . . .
        then the failing towns and the fostering
Cities fasten their lonely concrete around themselves:
Drowning inward toward their central emptiness:
                        isolated
As the vast high-pressure systems, anticyclonic mainsprings
Coil and uncurl and the great weatherclock rounds the seasons.
Then we may love man: so weak, so poor, in that
Cold wind . . .
        (where even the lights of the villages contract,
Abashed and afraid in the face of a thousand miles of ice,
Its white pall . . .)
        love him as we love all transient beings,
Brother and sister wildlings at home in that transhuman cold
That's not machine-made.
              Where all are even.
                 Then I'm at home.

But now, like clapboard clouds, the houses float over
The small towns in the tall white Christmas night . . .
                    lifted . . .

(Thin wrack of cloud, towering aloft, darkens
The high heavens but only slightly: the moon still silvers
Those little arks . . .)
                      lifting and drifting . . .
                                          a holy frivolity
Sustains them: swung on a rope of bellsound into the metallic
Light . . .
          joyfully . . .
                      in the joyful season . . .
                                          —this false peace.
Heavenly Levitation!
                      Man has put down his axe—
Now, if only a moment—and the peaceable kingdom exists:
As long as these souls and houses soar and sing: hoisted
By the rejoicing and hopeful bells . . .
                                          (As, now, the bells
Of that other Lisbon [Portugal] fall through the July snow
Of leaflets calling for the class war.)
                                    false
                                          Christmas
                                                peace.

V I.

In Transit:

Niño Perdido Toward Pah-Gatzin-Kay

REMEMBERING LOVES AND DEATHS

They happened in us . . .
But later we moved away—
Or they did.

Went west.
Went south to the goldfields.
Disappeared somewhere beyond Salt Lake or Denver—
Their roads are still in the map of our flesh:
Easy to get to almost any time
Around midnight.

But the land shifts and changes, the map
Gets out of date,
The century stretches its joints,
And one day we stand by the marked tree and ask: WAS IT HERE
WAS IT HERE
While, stunned but tireless,
Memory, the lodestone that always points toward pain
Hunts, slow and sluggish for its North,
Turning through the thickening crystals of tired flesh
That was pure honey, once.

FOR TOMASITO

Late in the early dark,
The little boy comes home.
A tear is in his eye,
From the cold—the cold
Of winter coming down.
But still he does not cry,

The little, happy, boy,
Because of cold—the cold
Is not within his heart.
It's not the mother dark
That hurts him till he cries.
The dying father sun
Puts darkness in his eyes.

CRAZY HORSE SAYS

Your parents set a great price on you.
But I would steal all the ponies of the Crows
For the sound of your flute once more.

FOR S.

I visit you seldom:
The night is so short
For dream migrants.
And I am afraid of forgetting
The long hard way home.

136

FAIRY STORY

I kissed the sleeping Princess. As in old
Fairy tales she woke. This made me bold.
I kissed her twice. She opened wide. And then
(And then): I kissed her thrice. She fell asleep again.

FOR NAOMI REPLANSKY

Writing in a dim light,
We feel the cold wind
From farther than Van Dieman's Land.
But the flame does not
Waver.

FOR DAVID JOHNSON GALLATIN CUMBERLAND

Midnight or noon
The poem flies past
Full of open places
Small campfires
And silence . . .
Ourselves the same—
Following.

WHY THE BLIND MUST REFUSE GUIDES
for Lyla Larson

When we were young it was the children—
They led us to middle age.
Then the adults helped us.
And we never got home again.

FOR DAVID MARTINSON AT DULUTH

It's good
When the last ice fades out on the waters
Like the worn unreadable pages of old notebooks.
Then our footprints
Can no longer go on without us.

FOR A BOOK BY CHARLES HUMBOLDT

Go forth bright book:
Thou art the shade
Of him who made thee.
He is stayed.

Take this book, Friend:
It has the power
To blaze trail
In a dark hour.

So, straying here,
We are not lost:
This shade gives light
To a nightbound host.

"THE HORSE NATIONS IN THEIR LEATHER TOWNS . . ."
for Jeff Jentz

The days go by . . .
They're like spotted horses!
Calicoes,
Appaloosas,
Indian ponies,
Outlaws . . .

> *Never been a horse what cain't be rode,*
> *Never been a man what cain't be throwed!*

Still: they can't all be bad!

FOR JACK BEECHING

They say we take things
Too lightly!
But it's skating on thin ice
That puts the spring in our walk!

GULLIVER'S TRAVELS
for Fred Manfred

It wasn't just that he was tall
But that he made us feel
We had lived all our life
On our knees.

WHERE WE'RE AT
for Tony Oldknow

Twelve years on the trail together!
Are we half way into
Or half way out
of the woods?

FOR DALE JACOBSON

After a long time in the closed cities of books
We go out into the sunlight . . .
—Even the shallowest river is deep!

As we look off over the trees at the hills
We become dizzy,
Drunk on the wine of emptiness and space.

FOR MY AUNT, JULIA SHEA

In the brilliant sun of the white solstice
A few snow crystals fall out of the clear sky . . .
Each of them, for no reason I can understand,
Seems a constellation of pure and icy joy.

THE WORLD; THE LOVERS; FALLING STARS
for Alice

Peaked in an immortal flame
The mortal moth-like lovers burn.
The love that sets their limbs alight
(Searing the snow of breast and thigh)
Can have no history but to die,
Yet cannot change. Across the night
Radiance of falling stars is borne:
Impermanent. These are the same
Who burn in the contradictions of
The strict and sensual laws of love.

Passing a point of no return,
An age consumed in instant flame,
The lovers cannot save themselves.
Bound in a swift triumphant arc,
Like falling stars, they light the dark
And loveless world. From private hells
All common daily good is torn,
Without history or name
Almost: though brilliance in the air
Lingers when a star was there.

THANKSGIVING, 1979

All over my body
Eyelids are opening.
But the eyes turn
                    inward:
To see many strange rocks with sharp edges;
And something small that moves around in the darkness . . . .

FROM A LONG WAY OUT OF PAH-GATZIN-KAY

With all those I love
Shining
In radiant light
On the other side of the world,
I lie down in this
Darkness.
I straighten my legs.
I close my eyes.
I try to dream of my own waking.
I hold myself in my own arms like a dead friend.

DON'T THINK YOU KNOW MY NAME!

And so I am getting old!
Like a tree in the forest
I am shedding branches and leaves, and around my feet
Are enough dry twigs for three English martyrs—
And every son-of-a-bitch wants to set me on fire. . . .

Not important of course. I'll have to walk out in the snow
In any case. Where else is there to turn?
So if you see me coming, a man made out of ice,
Splintering light like rainbows at every crazed joint of my body,
Better get out of the way: this black blood won't burn
And the fierce acids of winter are smoking in this cold heart.

THE WAY I LIVE NOW

Crippled or not
(Now that I limp)
I notice the others . . .
One glance of recognition
And we go on . . .
        and on . . .
                on . . .

POEM

My little son comes running with open arms!
Sometimes I can't bear it,
Father.
Did I, too,
Open your heart almost to breaking?

ROUND SONG

My dead father comes back
In the shape of my little son.

And I sing him to sleep with his songs
Still in my own child's ear.

AFTER A DEATH

Dead for a year, mother . . .
And my heart—still!—
Keeps turning
Turning to the west
Whenever I have news to tell.

ON MOVING INTO A NEW HOUSE

Guardian spirits of Earth and Air,
Smile on the limits of this pair
Who, from old and boundless night
Cast out, in these calm confines of light
Rest for a little: pilgrims come
To a junction of the times and Time.

Holy and eternal fire,
Here curb the range of thy Empire.
Kindle these tinder souls to learn
The Light: though fevered cities burn.
Bless this hearth; instruct these two
To live as salamanders do.

Creation's font, O perilous flood
Contain thy tide within the blood
And bless. Beneath the fingernail
Vast oceanic hells prevail,
And monsters of chaos. Gentle these
To man-framed forms and energies.

Let no remembered ghost, though dear,
Trouble this close; nor enter here
(However assured of mortal home)
Demon familiars. Guide through storm
This earthbound windjammer, burning Ark,
Across the salt gulfs of the dark.

144

JOURNEYS

Sometime on the long voyage back
The sea entered my body,
Stealthy, female and full of recognitions.

Now, two months returned to the flat prairie,
It still lives in my flesh.

Perhaps I shall spend the rest of my life
In an open boat
Drifting
Far far from land.

NIGHT SONG

Midnight, and day's end;
But who can say amen?

He who would prey or slay
Has prospered all the day.

She who would only love
Now whores on the cold grave,

Grieving. I sing alone.
The absolution of song

Falls on the inner ear—
But they do not hear or care.

(Still, I cannot blame—
Would bless if I could,

Who know how the world drives
Past all that soul can bear.)

I sing them a cold theme
(Made from the faithless moon)

Of indifference and joy,
Joy and indifference,

Made as I make this poem
From the eternal and time,

From midnight and day's end.
Made to say Amen

To the lovers and murderers
In life's holy orders,

Wantons who curse or bless
The stations of their dust—

As I write or make love:
To keep the night alive.

EVERYTHING IN ORDER

I'll never get to where I'm going!
No surprise in that . . .
Plugging through this deep snow,
My arms heavy with the weight of the dead . . .

THERE'LL BE SOME CHANGES MADE

All month long I have heard the owls
Floating their heavy lumber through the dark.
They are building an extra room
On the night.

HOMAGE

To sit just downslope from the brow of a low hill
In the early evening.
To wait for the second song of the cricket—
What a great teacher you were
O my beloved father!

NIGHT WORK

It's too much: this hard work—
All night chipping on the stone of sleep . . .

And then to wake in the morning
And find only the old, known,
Statue of solitude—
Hardly changed at all . . .

WHAT WAKES US

It was no dream—
Those great black doors
Rushing toward us
Through the night . . .

LIVING ON FAITH

A statistical statement of destiny assumes
(Or the Principle According to Heisenberg means)
(Or probably means) it's merely probable
The air in my room or in my world
Won't suddenly congregate under the bed,
Or in empty places in a book or a head
Or go into a reservation in some dark corner or continent.
And then would all our clamoring flags be furled!
Such change would be only chancy, not devilish or wanton.

It's a breath-taking idea!
For a moment I inhale the delicious consternation of time-tables!
Weightless in the serious comedy of a farout and funky gravity,
(Or gassed by reversals, where the poor are enriched by laughter
As the Bishop, pneumatic with spirit, is squashed flat)
Counting my breath and inventing these charming fables
I wait for the bankers to fly off like charmed quarks.
But they lack charm or are too weighty to fly
(Getting or spending they've no time for larks)
Until such time as the Poor can move them—
And just now the Poor are too poor in spirit to try.
So, preparing a reversal of gravity, I wait.

Meanwhile this rock and that bird don't seem to care
About statistical statements of destiny.
Flying or falling they have about them an air
That's jaunty with faith: the world is what comes next,
They seem to say. And I, who'd be debonair,
Swim up out of these depths inspired
To take a deep breath of whatever's out there.

148

TRIUMPHAL MARCH

After the long strike
We continued walking in circles
For a long time: dreaming:
Many nights many days
Dizzy (but not with success)
From the round dance of our struggle!

O Solidarity!
What did it matter we'd lost?

MYSTERY

Now the old year burns away
To alarums of a joyous bell.
The old king dies. From his cold Hell
The kingly stranger comes, to play

His double game. Disguises work
To hide from us his constant face.
Masked, the New Year takes its place,
And starts, like the old one, in the dark.

THE RETURN

The trees are never the same
                      twice
                          the animals
                                    the birds or
The little river lying on its back in the sun or the sun or
The varying moon changing over the changing hills
Constant.
             It is this, still, that most I love about them.

I enter by dark or day:
                    that green noise, dying
Alive and living its death, that inhuman circular singing,
May call me stranger . . .
                      Or the little doors of the bark open
And I enter that other home outside the tent of my skin . . .

On such days, on such midnights, I have gone, I will go,
Past the human, past the animal, past the bird,
To the old mothers who stand with their feet in the loamy dark
And their green and gold praises playing into the sun . . .

For a little while, only. (It is a long way back.)
But at least, and if but for a moment, I have almost entered the stone.
Then fear and love call. I am cast out. Alien,
On the bridge of fur and of feather I go back to the world I have known.

Thomas McGrath was born on a farm in North Dakota in 1916. He attended the University of North Dakota, Louisiana State University and New College, and Oxford University where he was a Rhodes Scholar. He served in the Air Force in the Aleutians during World War II. He has taught at colleges and universities in Maine, California, New York, North Dakota, and Minnesota.

He has held the Amy Lowell Travelling Poetry Scholarship, 1966-67, received a Guggenheim Fellowship, 1967-68, a Bush Foundation Fellowship, 1976-77, and an NEA Fellowship, 1982.

He is the author of *Letter to an Imaginary Friend* (Parts I and II), *The Movie at the End of the World*: Collected Poems, and other books. He founded and was the first editor (with Eugenia McGrath) of the poetry magazine *Crazy Horse*. He has a son, Tomasito, age 12.